A CELEBRATION OF

DAVID ATTENBOROUGH

The Activity Book

D1148468

A CELEBRATION OF

DAVID ATTENBOROUGH
The Activity Book

NATHAN JOYCE

ILLUSTRATIONS BY PETER JAMES FIELD

PORTICO

First published in the United Kingdom in 2018 by
Portico
43 Great Ormond Street
London
WC1N 3HZ

An imprint of Pavilion Books Company Ltd

ISBN 978-1-91162-212-3

A CIP catalogue record for this book is available from the British Library.

10 9 8 7 6 5 4 3 2 1

Reproduction by Rival Colour Ltd, UK
Printed and bound by CPI Group (UK) Ltd, Croydon, CR0 4YY

This book can be ordered direct from the publisher at
www.pavilionbooks.com

CONTENTS

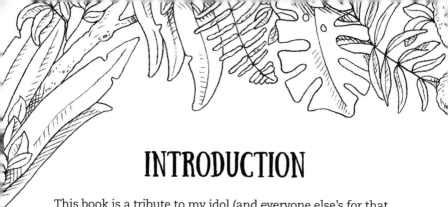

INTRODUCTION

This book is a tribute to my idol (and everyone else's for that matter), who captivated me aged seven when I first saw *The Trials of Life*. David's sitting down on a rock on a Christmas Island beach while millions of red crabs clamber past him. Well, I say 'past' him. Most of them try to clamber over him. He remains characteristically unflappable and his passion and boundless energy fill the screen as much as the crabs do.

There are few situations that David's soothing tones would not improve. Captain and First Officer unconscious in cockpit? It's OK, Attenborough's on board. He'll figure it out and get the plane down calmly. Can't put together that Ikea furniture? Just ask yourself what would Attenborough do. The 7:18 train from Brighton to Victoria is delayed (again)? Suddenly David voices the apologetic announcement. Everyone feels better. And they remember to recycle too.

And despite David's cultural crown jewel status, he didn't even reach the podium when the public was asked to name Britain's polar research vessel in 2016. How is

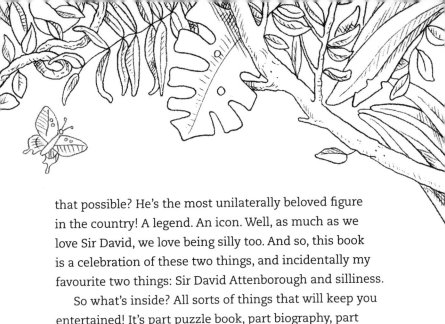

that possible? He's the most unilaterally beloved figure in the country! A legend. An icon. Well, as much as we love Sir David, we love being silly too. And so, this book is a celebration of these two things, and incidentally my favourite two things: Sir David Attenborough and silliness.

So what's inside? All sorts of things that will keep you entertained! It's part puzzle book, part biography, part fascinating fact book ('Species Named in David's Honour'), part quiz book ('The Ultimate Nature Quiz') and part ridiculously silly activity book (design a new shirt for Sir David in 'Patternborough').

And there's the occasional serious bit on an infographic. Because at the heart of everything Sir David does is a vital message. We live on an extraordinary planet and must protect it and its remarkable diversity for future generations. And like Sir David, there's no reason we can't have fun while we're doing it.

GUESS THE ANIMALS

Can you guess the animals David's talking about?

1 *'It looks like a survivor from the age of the dinosaurs. Huge claws and 60 serrated teeth can cause terrible damage.'*

A Giant Anteater

B Komodo Dragon

C Cassowary

D Nine-banded Armadillo

2 *'He's going to have to use trickery. He tones down his colours and tucks in his arms. He's just the right size to mimic a female.'*

A Giant Cuttlefish

B Panther Chameleon

C Winged Seahorse

D North American Tree Frog

3 *'Walking on thin ice is always risky. And it's hard to retain one's dignity, especially when you're wearing stilts.'*

A Arctic Hare

B Andean Flamingo

C Reindeer

D Snow Goose

4 *'He's only the size of a pencil and he eats ants … He can travel over 100 feet in a single leap.'*

A Draco (Flying) Lizard

B Horse Lubber Grasshopper

C Zebra Black Spider

D Panamanian Golden Frog

5 *'One of the most voracious nocturnal predators is also one of the hardest to see. This mysterious creature hardly ever appears on the surface of the dunes. It's no bigger than a ping-pong ball.'*

A African Pygmy Hedgehog

B Carpenter Ant

C Tiger Beetle

D Golden Mole

6 *'It only does it once a week, but why does it come down to the ground to do it? And why does it nearly always choose to do it in exactly the same place?'* (Bonus point for the activity David is talking about.)

A Olive Baboon

B Peruvian Spider Monkey

C Green Tree Python

D Three-toed Sloth

7 *'This family is resting between bouts of feeding. Who knows what the owners of the biggest brain in the planet dream about.'*

A Sperm Whale

B African Elephant

C Killer Whale

D Bottlenose Dolphin

8 *'The young male aims for the rump. The old bull targets his rival's legs. The old bull is down. Is this the end of his reign? He knows a knockout blow is coming. But the old bull ducks, and strikes a blow to his rival's underbelly. Out for the count. The old bull is victorious, but only just.'*

A Giraffe

B African Elephant

C Common Hippo

D Red Kangaroo

(Answers on page 187.)

WIT & WISDOM
FUNNY QUOTES

'Well I'm having a good time.
Which makes me feel guilty.
How very English.'

(On the perils of Britishness.)

'I suggested a documentary on geology,
but it never got off the ground!'

(It turns out David has a penchant for puns.)

'I just love a good leaf.'

(And who doesn't?)

'The problem with rats is they would run the
place given half the chance, and I've had them
leap out of a lavatory while I've been sitting on it.'

(On his least favourite creature.)

'About 70 or 80 men jumped onto the track, brandishing knives and spears. To say I was alarmed is to put it mildly... I walked towards this screaming horde of men, I stuck out my hand, and I heard myself say "Good afternoon."'

(The personification of calm when confronted by a tribe of armed cannibals.)

'We could shoot him ... It's not a bad idea ...'

(On what to do about Donald Trump.)

THE MOST TRUSTED PEOPLE

OnePoll.com surveyed 2,000 Britons in January 2018 to discover which celebrity was the most trustworthy. I applaud them for their sensible decision-making. The top ten were:

1. David Attenborough
2. Tom Hanks
3. Michelle Obama
4. Prince William
5. The Queen
6. Morgan Freeman
7. Prince Harry
8. Stephen Hawking
9. Barack Obama
10. Judi Dench

PUZZLES

1 Sir David's full name (plus titles) is

Sir David Frederick Attenborough, OM, CH, CVO, CBE, FRS, FLS, FZS, FSA

How many letters of the alphabet are not included above and what are they?

2 Which Attenborough magic moment involved the sound of a camera shutter, then a car with its alarm going off, and finally a chainsaw?

(Answers on page 187.)

THE ORDER OF MERIT

Founded in 1902 by King Edward VII, the Order of Merit honours exceptional service in science, art, literature or in public service. The exclusive order is restricted to only 24 members and allows members to use the letters OM after their name. After receiving the honour, Sir David said:

'How could anyone believe they actually deserved something like this?'

Legend. The current holders are:

	NAME	OCCUPATION	DATE OF APPOINTMENT
1	The Duke of Edinburgh	...	10 June 1968
2	Sir Michael Atiyah	Mathematician	17 November 1992
3	Sir Aaron Klug	Biophysicist	23 October 1995
4	Norman Foster, Baron Foster of Thames Bank	Architect	25 November 1997
5	Sir Roger Penrose	Physicist	9 May 2000
6	Sir Tom Stoppard	Playwright	9 May 2000
7	The Prince of Wales	...	27 June 2002
8	Robert May, Baron May of Oxford	Ecologist	28 October 2002
9	Jacob Rothschild, The Lord Rothschild	Philanthropist	28 October 2002

10	Sir David Attenborough	**General hero**	10 June 2005
11	Betty Boothroyd, The Baroness Boothroyd	Former Speaker of the House of Commons	10 June 2005
12	Sir Michael Howard	Historian	10 June 2005
13	Robin Eames, The Lord Eames	Former Primate of All Ireland	13 June 2007
14	Sir Tim Berners-Lee	Inventor of the World Wide Web	13 June 2007
15	Martin John Rees, The Lord Rees of Ludlow	Astronomer Royal	13 June 2007
16	Jean Chrétien	Former Prime Minister of Canada	13 July 2009
17	Neil MacGregor	Historian	4 November 2010
18	David Hockney	Artist	1 January 2012
19	John Howard	Former Prime Minister of Australia	1 January 2012
20	Sir Simon Rattle	Conductor	1 January 2014
21	Sir Magdi Yacoub	Surgeon	1 January 2014
22	Ara Darzi, The Lord Darzi of Denham	Surgeon	31 December 2015
23	Dame Ann Dowling	Engineer	31 December 2015
24	Sir James Dyson	Inventor	31 December 2015

SPECIES NAMED IN DAVID'S HONOUR

Attenborosaurus

Twenty different species (and one entire genus) have been named for David. Unbelievably, that only puts him in bronze-medal position on the all-time list, behind Alexander von Humboldt and Charles Darwin (what did he ever do, anyway?). There's still time, though …

SCIENTIFIC NAME	DESCRIPTION	YEAR DESCRIBED
Attenborosaurus conybeari	An ancient long-necked marine reptile originally identified as a plesiosaurus	1993
Zaglossus attenboroughi	Long-beaked echidna (critically endangered spiny anteater)	1998
Materpiscis attenboroughi	Extinct armoured fish (approx. 380m-year-old specimen from Australia)	2008
Blakea attenboroughi	Ecuadorian flowering tree	2009
Nepenthes attenboroughii	Attenborough's pitcher plant (carnivorous plant that can digest rats and shrews)	2009
Ctenocheloides attenboroughi	Ghost shrimp (small, transparent shrimp found in Madagascar)	2010
Prethopalpus attenboroughi	Goblin spider (just over 1mm long)	2012
Polioptila attenboroughi	Inambari gnatcatcher (small Peruvian bird)	2013
Electrotettix attenboroughi	Extinct pygmy locust (approx. 20m years old)	2014

Trigonopterus attenboroughi	Flightless weevil (type of beetle from Indonesia; just over 2mm long)	2014
Sirdavidia	Entire genus (taxonomic category above species) of flowering plants with pink petals and yellow stems	2015
Hieracium attenboroughianum	Alpine hawkweed (type of wild flower; only living British species to be named after David)	2015
Platysaurus attenboroughi	Attenborough's flat lizard (brightly coloured lizard from Namibia/South Africa)	2015
Euptychia attenboroughi	Attenborough's black-eyed satyr (rare brown and orange butterfly with distinctive black spots)	2016
Microleo attenboroughi	Extinct miniature marsupial lion (approx. 19m years old)	2016
Attenborougharion rubicundus	Species of semi-slug from Tasmania	2017
Pristimantis attenboroughi	Attenborough's rubber frog (found in the Peruvian Andes and classed as endangered)	2017
Cascolus ravitis	Extinct shrimp (approx. 430m-year-old specimen found in volcanic ash; 'cascolus' is a Latin rendering of the Old English equivalent to 'Attenborough')	2017
Mesosticta davidattenboroughi	Extinct damselfly (approx. 70m-year-old specimen found in fossilised amber in Myanmar)	2017
Acisoma attenboroughi	Attenborough's pintail (a common dragonfly from Madagascar)	2017
Sitana attenboroughii	Attenborough's fan-throated lizard (found in Kerala, southwestern India)	2018

ATTENBOROUGH FIELD NOTES
THE EARLY YEARS

- David was born on 8 May 1926.

- David grew up in College House on what is now part of the campus of the University of Leicester. His father, Frederick, was the principal of what was then University College, Leicester, and has a building – the 18-storey Attenborough Tower – named after him.

- His elder brother Richard once locked David in a padded cell inside the Fielding Johnson Building at the university, which had been built as a lunatic asylum and was later used as a military hospital.

- The young David spent a lot of time collecting fossils and created a 'museum' at his family home. Shortly after the writer and archaeologist Jacquetta Hawkes visited the house and admired David's collection, she sent him a parcel including a dried sea horse, a piece of Roman pottery and an Anglo-Saxon coin. This spurred David on to become a naturalist.

- When he turned eight, his father gave David a fire salamander as a birthday present.

- When David was ten, a Native American conservation pioneer by the name of Grey Owl* came to De Montfort Hall in Leicester to give a talk about protecting the habitat of the beaver in the Canadian wilderness and man's impact on the flora and fauna of North America. David was inspired and managed to get one of Grey Owl's books signed by the author.

- Aged 11, the enterprising young David sold newts he'd collected to the university for 3d (three old pence – about 1p) each. They came from a pond only five metres away from the zoology department.

- At age 13, David cycled from Leicester to the Lake District and back again, collecting fossils and staying in youth hostels. He was away for three weeks, and his mother and father didn't know where he was!

- Aged 16, when he was supposed to be in school studying Latin, David took trains to listen to zoology lectures at the University of Nottingham.

---

* Grey Owl was born Archibald Belaney in Hastings, UK. After his death in 1938 he was exposed for lying about his Native American heritage.

ATTENBOROUGH CONSTELLATION DOT-TO-DOT

In December 2017, astronomers at the University of Birmingham devised new star alignments to honour eight iconic figures. They showed Usain Bolt (in his 'lightning bolt' pose), Mo Farah (doing the Mobot), a book to represent Malala Yousafzai, a tennis racket for Serena Williams, a space shuttle for astronaut Tim Peake, a pair of glasses for Harry Potter, and a pair of wellington boots for Paddington Bear. A whale was chosen to represent the eighth member of this illustrious group – our very own Sir David. Slightly odd decision. I would have gone for a great grey owl.

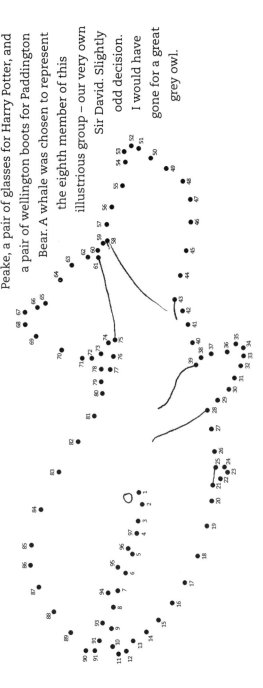

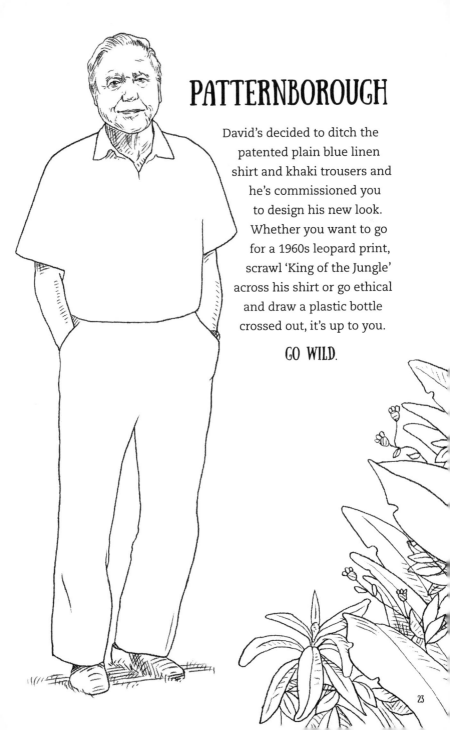

PATTERNBOROUGH

David's decided to ditch the patented plain blue linen shirt and khaki trousers and he's commissioned you to design his new look. Whether you want to go for a 1960s leopard print, scrawl 'King of the Jungle' across his shirt or go ethical and draw a plastic bottle crossed out, it's up to you.

GO WILD.

THE DAVID ATTENBOROUGH DRINKING GAME

'Once again very many thanks to you both from Geoff and from me. We will never forget the time we spent with you. If you come to England you must, of course, write and let me know so that we can organise a little drinking session ...'

(Letter from David to an associate in Fiji, 1 January 1960.)

RULES Plonk yourself down in front of any one of his spectacular documentaries and assemble a group of ne'er-do-wells and a fairly large quantity of ale.

ONE GLUG each time David mentions the following words:

'CREATURE'	'PREDATOR'
'ANIMAL'	'PREY'
'SUN'	'SPECIES'
'YOUNG'	'MALE'
'FOOD'	'FEMALE'

so it's two glugs every time I say 'known to man.'

TWO GLUGS every time David utters one of the following:

'IN THE WORLD'   'KNOWN TO MAN'

'ON THE PLANET'   'EXTRAORDINARY'

'ALL OF US'   'MIRACULOUS'

DOWN YOUR DRINK each time David addresses the camera.

ATTENBOGGLE

How many words can you find on the Boggle board below?
Only words of four or more letters please!

(Answers on page 187.)

DAVID'S UNOFFICIAL GYM PLAYLIST

Africa Toto

Norwegian Wood The Beatles

I Am the Walrus The Beatles

Octopus's Garden The Beatles

Blackbird The Beatles

Hungry Like the Wolf Duran Duran

When Doves Cry Prince

The Lion Sleeps Tonight The Tokens

The Sidewinder Sleeps Tonite R.E.M.

Union of the Snake Duran Duran

Surfin' Bird The Trashmen

Crocodile Rock Elton John

Three Lions The Lightning Seeds

Eye of the Tiger Survivor

Superfast Jellyfish Gorillaz

Disloyal Order of Water Buffaloes Fall Out Boy

Unfinished Monkey Business Ian Brown

Who's Gonna Ride Your Wild Horses U2

Wolf Like Me TV On The Radio

Buffalo Soldier Bob Marley

Feel free to add any suggestions!

ULTIMATE DINNER PARTY GUEST LIST

You've been given the chance to invite any six people, living or dead, to a dinner party.

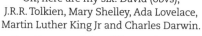

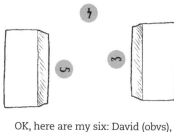

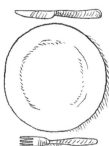

OK, here are my six: David (obvs), J.R.R. Tolkien, Mary Shelley, Ada Lovelace, Martin Luther King Jr and Charles Darwin.

Fine, I'm a nerd, but I'd love to hear an Attenborough/Darwin chinwag. Fill out yours on this lovely table provided.

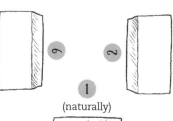

(naturally)

Sir David Attenborough

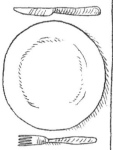

100 GREATEST BRITONS

Sir David was 63rd in the BBC's list of Greatest Britons, voted for by the public in 2002. That's an outrage, in my opinion. I think it's the taking a beating by Cliff Richard that really gets me. Special thank you to Michael Crawford, who very generously offered to count the votes.

1 Winston Churchill
2 Isambard Kingdom Brunel
3 Princess Diana
4 Charles Darwin
5 William Shakespeare
6 Isaac Newton
7 Elizabeth I
8 John Lennon
9 Lord Nelson
10 Oliver Cromwell
11 Ernest Shackleton
12 Captain James Cook
13 Robert Baden-Powell
14 Alfred the Great
15 Duke of Wellington
16 Margaret Thatcher
17 Michael Crawford
18 Queen Victoria
19 Paul McCartney
20 Alexander Fleming
21 Alan Turing
22 Michael Faraday
23 Owain Glyndŵr
24 Elizabeth II
25 Stephen Hawking
26 William Tyndale
27 Emmeline Pankhurst
28 William Wilberforce
29 David Bowie
30 Guy Fawkes
31 Leonard Cheshire
32 Eric Morecambe
33 David Beckham
34 Thomas Paine

35 Boudica
36 Steve Redgrave
37 Thomas More
38 William Blake
39 John Harrison
40 Henry VIII
41 Charles Dickens
42 Frank Whittle
43 John Peel
44 John Logie Baird
45 Aneurin Bevan
46 Boy George
47 Douglas Bader
48 William Wallace
49 Francis Drake
50 John Wesley
51 King Arthur
52 Florence Nightingale
53 T.E. Lawrence
54 Robert Falcon Scott
55 Enoch Powell
56 Cliff Richard
57 Alexander Graham Bell
58 Freddie Mercury
59 Julie Andrews
60 Edward Elgar
61 Queen Elizabeth the Queen Mother
62 George Harrison
63 **David Attenborough**
64 James Connolly
65 George Stephenson
66 Charlie Chaplin
67 Tony Blair

68 William Caxton
69 Bobby Moore
70 Jane Austen
71 William Booth
72 Henry V
73 Aleister Crowley
74 Robert the Bruce
75 Bob Geldof
76 The Unknown Warrior
77 Robbie Williams
78 Edward Jenner
79 David Lloyd George
80 Charles Babbage
81 Geoffrey Chaucer
82 Richard III
83 J.K. Rowling
84 James Watt
85 Richard Branson
86 Bono
87 John Lydon
88 Bernard Law Montgomery
89 Donald Campbell
90 Henry II
91 James Clerk Maxwell
92 J.R.R. Tolkien
93 Sir Walter Raleigh
94 Edward I
95 Barnes Wallis
96 Richard Burton
97 Tony Benn
98 David Livingstone
99 Tim Berners-Lee
100 Marie Stopes

CREATE YOUR OWN ATTENBOROUGH COAT OF ARMS

Here's the Attenborough family coat of arms and motto.
There's only one bloody animal on it! I think we can do
better than that, can't we? Please use the crest provided for
something more appropriate. And I think we need a motto
on the bottom rather than 'England', which looks like an
album filler at the moment.

FIND THE REAL SPECIES

Can you spot the real species lurking among this frankly ludicrous-sounding collection of animals?

1A White-tipped Goodnight Bird
1B White-finned Get-lost Bird
1C White-bellied Go-away Bird

2A Dik-dik
2B Nob-nob
2C Todger-todger

3A Agra Cadabra
3B Avada Kedavra
3C Alakazam

4A Holy-water Gecko
4B Satanic Leaf–tailed Gecko
4C Angelic Leaf-faced Gecko

(Answers on page 187.)

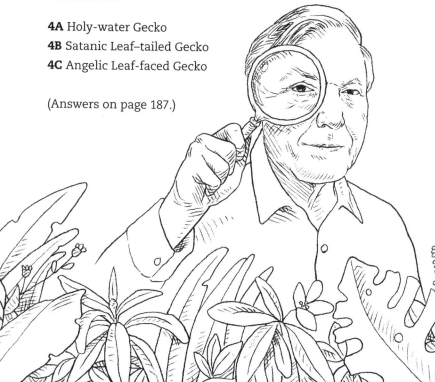

EVEN DAVID CAN MAKE MISTAKES

David's first appearance on television was to interview the largely monosyllabic Olympic long-distance runner Gordon Pirie. The interview was, by David's own admission, 'not a success'. However, it wasn't the slightly awkward nature of the interview that Mary Adams, David's first boss at the BBC Talks Department, dwelt on. She wrote in her notes:

> *'David Attenborough is intelligent and promising and may well be producer material, but he is not to be used again as an interviewer. His teeth are too big.'*

#THUGLIFE

David isn't exactly known for slamming other celebrities. This is just about the closest he's got to a rude remark: 'A small, vivacious, bird-like lady – though perhaps with rather more of the eagle than the wren,' (about Grace Wyndham Goldie, BBC Talks Department producer, who he writes about in his autobiography *Life on Air*.)

But in January 2018, David did speak out about reality show *The Island*, criticising Bear Grylls for killing animals purely for entertainment purposes:

'We've never killed an animal. Bear Grylls will have to answer for himself. But I wouldn't willingly kill an animal just to get a shot.'

And if David's upset, I think it's fair to say that the rest of the world is too.

TV AND FILM AWARDS

1962 British Academy Television Special Award
1970 British Academy Television Desmond Davis Award for Services to Television
1980 BAFTA Fellowship
1985 Royal Geographical Society Founder's Gold Medal
1985 International Emmy Founders Award, given by the International Academy of Television Arts and Sciences to individuals whose creative accomplishments have contributed in some way to the quality of global television production
2006 Special Recognition Award at the National Television Awards
2011 News & Documentary Emmy Award for Outstanding Nature Programming for *First Life*
2011 News & Documentary Emmy Award for Outstanding Writing for *First Life*
2011 BAFTA for Best Specialist Factual for *Flying Monsters 3D with David Attenborough*
2011 Association for International Broadcasting AIB International TV Personality of the Year
2014 BAFTA for Best Specialist Factual for *David Attenborough's Natural History Museum Alive*
2014 Personal Award at the George Foster Peabody Awards (distinguished achievement and meritorious public service by television and radio stations, networks, producing organisations, individuals and the World Wide Web)
2017 BAFTA for Best Specialist Factual for *Planet Earth II*
2018 National Television Award Impact Award for *Blue Planet II*

And many more to come …

BOATY McBOATFACE GATE

On 17 March 2016, the Natural Environment Research Council (NERC) asked the public to come up with a name for their new polar research vessel. And then all hell broke loose.

The runaway winner, with 124,109 votes, was *Boaty McBoatface*, a suggestion from former BBC Radio Jersey Presenter James Hand. Alas, *David Attenborough* limped home in fifth, with 10,284 votes, one place behind *It's Bloody Cold Here*.

Despite a public outcry, including one chap who wrote: 'If this boat isn't named *Boaty McBoatface*, then democracy has failed,' Boaty McBoatface was dropped in favour of our hero. And so the boat was christened the RRS (Royal Research Vessel) *David Attenborough*.

However, all was not lost. On 6 May 2016, British science minister Jo Johnson announced that a remotely operated submarine on board the RRS *David Attenborough* would be named *Boaty McBoatface*, something that David confirmed on ITV's *Good Morning Britain* on 17 October 2016.

Boaty successfully completed its inaugural mission in June 2017, and in March 2018 it undertook a two-month mission exploring a colossal ice shelf nearly 1km below the surface.

ATTENBOROUGH KARAOKE
'LET IT BE'

With a couple of minor adjustments, the lyrics to
The Beatles' 'Let it Be' are much more universal.

When you find yourself in times of
trouble, Attenborough comes to me
Speaking words of wisdom
Let it be

And in my hour of darkness
He is standing right in front of me
Speaking words of wisdom
Let it be

Let it be, let it be, let it be, let it be
Whisper words of wisdom
Let it be

And when the broken-hearted people
Living in the world agree
Attenborough will answer:
Let it be

For though they may be parted there is
Still a chance that they will see
Attenborough will answer
Let it be

Let it be, let it be, let it be, let it be
Yeah, Attenborough will answer
Let it be

Let it be, let it be, let it be, let it be
Whisper words of wisdom
Let it be

Let it be, let it be, let it be, let it be
Whisper words of wisdom
Let it be

And when the night is cloudy
There is still a light that shines on me
Shine until tomorrow
Let it be

I wake up to the sound of music
Attenborough comes to me
Speaking words of wisdom
Let it be

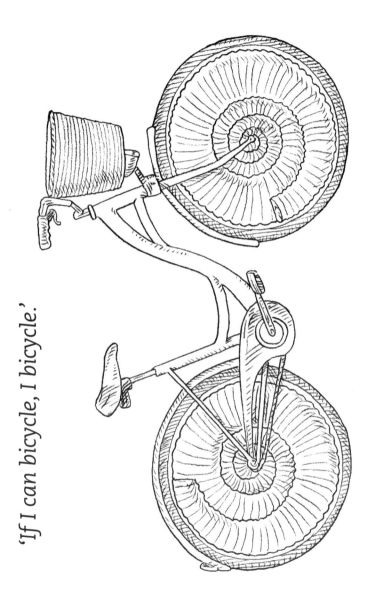

'If I can bicycle, I bicycle.'

GENUINE DANGER!

It's one of the most common questions posed to Sir David. Has he ever been in serious danger? Well, he did wrestle a wolf and got bitten by a python. But hey, no biggie.

PYTHON BITE

I've been bitten by a python.
Not a very big one. I was being silly,
saying: 'Oh, it's not poisonous …'
Then, wallop! But you have fear
around animals. If a king cobra came
in this room now, nine feet long and
rearing up to six feet tall, with a bite
that means certain death, and it can
move much faster than you can and
is not afraid of human beings and is
known to attack without provocation
… Yeah, I'd be on that table in a shot.

(Taken from a *Metro* interview on
Tuesday 29 January 2013.)

ATTEN'FROS

David's ditching the silver side parting and has hired you to help find him a new 'fro. Cut out your chosen style so we can add 'fashion icon' to his lengthy list of attributes.

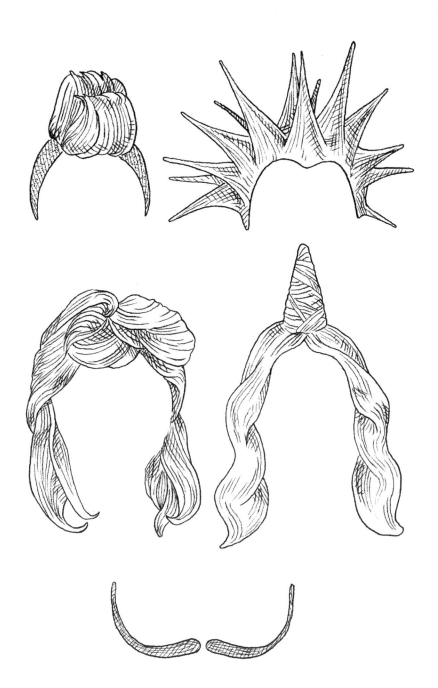

ATTENBOROUGH FIELD NOTES
EARLY ADULTHOOD

- David won a scholarship to study natural sciences at Clare College, Cambridge, in 1945. Of the intensive two-year degree, he said, 'If you read science, you didn't laze around on the river with girls – like people reading English and philosophy – but it was a paradisiacal time.'

- David served in the Home Guard during the Second World War, and compared himself to Private Pike from *Dad's Army* on account of his youth and role. David turned 19 on VE (Victory in Europe) Day, 1945 and remembers that 'we swarmed up and down ropes on the university buildings. What that represented I can't recall, but anyway that's what we did.'

- He was awarded a 2:1 degree and admitted that he found the three-dimensional crystallography part of the course tough.

- David was called up for national service in 1947 and served in the Royal Navy for two years. He hoped to be sent somewhere 'romantic', so was understandably delighted to undertake his preliminary training in Gosport. Despite expressing an interest to serve in the Far Eastern Fleet in Ceylon (Sri Lanka), he was sent to the Firth of Forth to serve on an aircraft carrier in the Reserve Fleet before it was mothballed.

- David had a climbing accident in the Lake District, falling between 30 and 40 feet, and felt absolutely sure that he was going to die. He thought of how sorry he was that he had let his parents down.

- In 1950, after his National Service was up, he decided he didn't want to study for a doctorate, feeling that the work was mostly laboratory-bound and not the way that he wanted to study animals.

- The same year, he married Jane Elizabeth Ebsworth Oriel. Their son Robert was born in 1951.

- David decided to try and get a job in publishing and became a junior editorial assistant with an educational publisher near St Paul's in London. He started on a book about tadpoles for primary schools. He said of his first job: 'Publishing was excruciatingly boring ... I thought, I can't do this for the rest of my life.'

- He was turned down (!) for his first job at the BBC, a producer in the radio Talks Department.

- All was not lost, though, as David got a telephone call from Mary Adams at the BBC's television service offering a three-month training course with no guarantee of employment afterwards. In his interview, David confessed to not having seen much television at all and not owning a set.

ATTENBOROUGH HIP-HOP ALBUM COVERS

One habitat that David hasn't explored yet is West Coast hip-hop. There's still time, though. So here's what would have happened if he'd taken up 50 Cent's offer and collaborated with him on his aptly named album *Animal Ambition*.

SOLVING THE BARNES MYSTERY

In July 2011, one of London's most gruesome unsolved murders, dubbed the 'Barnes Mystery', was solved. Thanks to Sir David.

On 2 March 1879, Julia Martha Thomas, a widow in her fifties from Richmond, was brutally murdered by her temporary cleaning lady Kate Webster, a 30-year-old Irishwoman on the run from the police after a number of theft convictions. In the midst of an argument, Webster threw Thomas down the stairs of her home and then choked her to death to prevent her from screaming. Webster decapitated and dismembered the body and boiled it, burning the bones in the hearth. It was alleged that Webster offered the boiled fat as dripping to local children, hence the name the 'Dripping Killer', although this has never been proven. Thomas's head was buried under the stables of the next-door pub, the Hole in the Wall.

At the time, the crime caused a sensation in England and Ireland. Even the Crown Prince of Sweden attended the trial at the Old Bailey. Webster was convicted and confessed before her execution but Thomas's head was never found during the initial investigation.

The Hole in the Wall pub had been derelict for over two years when David bought it in 2009 to prevent developers from building a block of flats there. David commissioned contractors to excavate the former pub, and they discovered a dark circular object that turned out to be a skull of a middle-aged woman.

In July 2011, carbon dating aged the skull to somewhere between 1650 and 1880. Analysis of the fracture marks on the skull were consistent with being thrown down the stairs, and the low collagen levels of the bone pointed to it having been boiled. The coroner concluded that the skull was that of Julia Martha Thomas and recorded a verdict of unlawful killing, replacing the original open verdict from 1879.

WIT & WISDOM
FUNNY QUOTES

'I had to climb up a pile of bat poo. And I got to the top and I was choking with ammonia. And the director said, howling up because he was at the bottom: "Say something!" So I said: "A lot of people are frightened of bats. A lot of people think they're going to tangle your hair. Not so, because of echolocation." The camera director said "Cut!" and the cameraman put the light out, and a bat hit me straight in the face.'

(Practice and preaching not quite in alignment.)

'You know, it's a terrible thing to appear on television, because people think you actually know what you're talking about.'

(It seems that even David suffers from imposter syndrome.)

'The thing about a bush baby is that the male establishes its territory by peeing on his hands and putting it all on the walls. And after you've had a pair for about six months, you can see people coming into the house, sniffing and going: "Now, that's definitely not mulligatawny soup."'

(Revealing David's lunchtime soup of choice.)

'Because I know it least and because I can get decent food and a reasonable bottle of cheap wine.'

(On why his favourite filming location is central Europe.)

'I expect I shall deal with it in a professional manner.'

(When asked what he would do if he was confronted by a polar bear.)

47

HATTENBOROUGH

David's off on a world tour and needs appropriate headgear.
Choose a hat, cut it out and add it to his glorious brain holder.

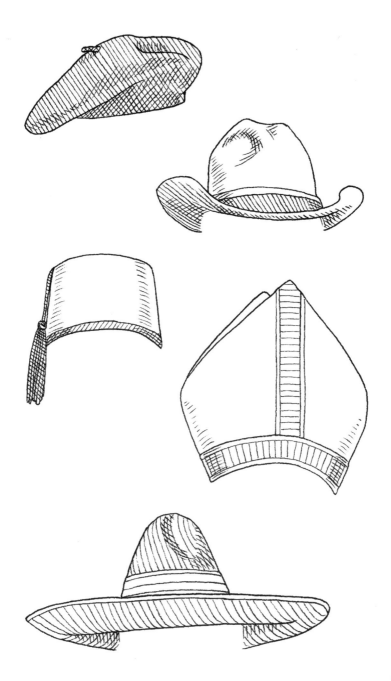

FAVOURITE ATTENBOROUGH MOMENTS

In 2006 a poll was conducted by the documentary television channel UKTV to find the public's favourite moment in David's 50-year broadcasting career. Here are the results.

1	David watching a lyrebird mimicking bird calls and man-made sounds including a camera shutter, a car alarm and a chainsaw	*The Life of Birds*
2	David up close with mountain gorillas in Rwanda	*Life on Earth*
3	David very excitedly observes a blue whale surfacing alongside his boat	*The Life of Mammals*
4	David describes the fall of the Rapa Nui civilisation on Easter Island	*State of the Planet*
5	Chimpanzees using stones to crack nuts open	*The Life of Mammals*
6	David with a grizzly bear behind him catching salmon	*The Life of Mammals*
7	David successfully imitating the sound of a Magellanic woodpecker drilling a hole in a tree trunk	*The Life of Birds*
8	Being tripped up by a displaying (and rather randy) male capercaillie	*The Life of Birds*

9	Chimpanzees wading through water on two legs	*The Life of Mammals*
10	A male Vogelkop bowerbird's collecting colourful objects	*Attenborough in Paradise*
11	Elephants mining salt in a Kenyan mountain cave	*The Life of Mammals*
12	Troop of chimpanzees using teamwork to chase and kill a colobus monkey	*The Trials of Life*
13	Mexican free-tailed bats leaving a cave and David freeing a young one	*The Trials of Life*
14	David being rounded on by a bellowing male elephant seal	*Life in the Freezer*
15	David with a wandering albatross feeding its chick	*Life in the Freezer*
16	The migration of 100 million Christmas Island red crabs	*The Trials of Life*
17	David in the forest canopy watching gibbons close up	*The Life of Mammals*
18	Burrowing under a termite mound to show how its ventilation system works	*The Trials of Life*
19	David describing titan arum (corpse flower), the world's largest flower	*The Private Life of Plants*
20	Timelapse footage of brambles growing and extending their territory	*The Private Life of Plants*

GUESS THE ANIMALS

Can you guess the animals David's talking about?

1 *'What kind of creature could be responsible for creating such a gruesome scene? There's a mysterious killer at work in this desert.'*
A African Wild Dog
B Butcherbird
C Inland Taipan
D Deathstalker Scorpion

2 *'It's huge, three metres across and addicted to lying on its side at the surface. It eats vast quantities of jellyfish.'*
A Atlantic Sailfish
B Yellowfin Tuna
C Manta Ray
D Sunfish

3 *'It has an ancestry that stretches back more than four hundred million years. It's a metre long. It tastes for scent. And feels for movement.'*
A Amazonian Giant Centipede
B Black Mamba
C Bobbit
D Monitor Lizard

4 *'They had to do something even more radical. They had to swim. They even learned to dive. They acquired the ability to hold their breath for up to an hour, so that they could swim down to a depth of 20 metres.'*
A Emperor Penguin
B Guillemot
C Marine Iguana
D Feral Pig

5 'It floats with the help of a gas-filled bladder, topped by a vertical membrane. With that serving as a sail, it maintains a steady course through the waves.'

A Box Jellyfish

B Portuguese Man o' War

C Loggerhead Sea Turtle

D Blobfish

6 'His luck may be in. The seduction can now begin. He's showing off his best goods. "Perhaps a little plastic piping? Or maybe a bit of coloured string?" But his guest doesn't seem to be paying much attention. "A fork, madame?" Nothing seems to be working … It's not easy finding sex in the city.'

A Great Bowerbird

B Common Green Magpie

C Burrowing Owl

D Black Kite

7 'Each of their heads weighs as much as a car. They have been duelling for days. Now in its third day, the contest is reaching a climax. Soon, one will be forced to concede.'

A African Elephant

B Giraffe

C Common Hippo

D Blue Whale

(Answers on page 187.)

8 'These sabre-toothed sausages wouldn't last a day in the desert. They have lost their fur. And most bizarrely, they live in social colonies, much like termites or ants.'

A Aye-Aye

B Star-nosed Mole

C Hairless Syrian Hamster

D Naked Mole Rat

DOT-TO-DOT
DAVID

Join the dots to
unite David with his
ring-tailed friend.

EMOTIONAL ROLLER COASTER

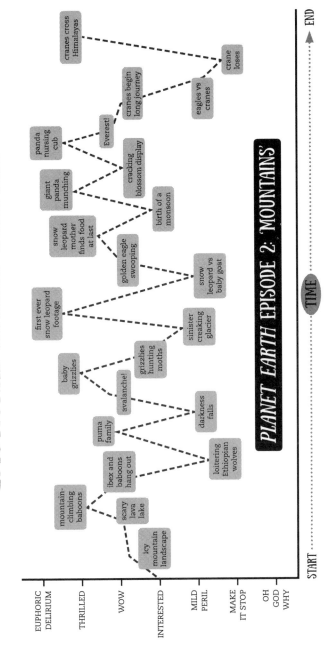

PLANET EARTH EPISODE 2: 'MOUNTAINS'

EUPHORIC
DELIRIUM

THRILLED

WOW

INTERESTED

MILD
PERIL

MAKE
IT STOP

OH
GOD
WHY

START

TIME

END

icy mountain landscape
mountain-climbing baboons
scary lava lake
ibex and baboons hang out
puma family
loitering Ethiopian wolves
avalanche!
darkness falls
baby grizzlies
grizzlies hunting moths
first ever snow leopard footage
sinister creaking glacier
snow leopard vs baby goat
golden eagle swooping
snow leopard mother finds food at last
birth of a monsoon
giant panda munching
cracking blossom display
panda nursing cub
Everest!
cranes begin long journey
eagles vs cranes
cranes cross Himalayas
crane loses

55

DESERT ISLAND DISCS CHOICES

David has appeared on Radio Four's *Desert Island Discs* four times, a record he shares with comedian Arthur Askey.

DAVID'S FIRST APPEARANCE 6 MAY 1957
Music choices

1 Ottilie Patterson: 'Trouble in Mind'

2 Johann Sebastian Bach: *Partita for Solo Violin No. 3 in E major* – 'Prelude'

3 Albert Ketèlbey: 'Stars and Stripes Forever'

4 Franz Schubert: *String Quintet in C major*

5 Henri Salvador: 'Maladie D'Amour'

6 George Frideric Handel: 'Haste thee, nymph' (from *L'Allegro, il penseroso ed il moderato*)

7 Jean Sibelius: *Tapiola*

8 Ralph Vaughan Williams: The Old Hundredth psalm tune, 'All people that on earth do dwell'

Luxury choice Piano

DAVID'S SECOND APPEARANCE 10 MARCH 1979
Music choices

1 George Frideric Handel: 'The Lord Is My Light' (Chandos Anthem No. 10)

2 Ludwig van Beethoven: *Symphony No. 2 in D major*

3 Johann Sebastian Bach/Busoni: *Partita for Solo Violin No. 2 in D minor* – 5th movement (Chaconne)

4 **Wolfgang Amadeus Mozart: 'Soave sia il vento' from *Cosi fan tutte* (favourite)**

5 Igor Stravinsky: *The Firebird*

6 Jan Dismas Zelenka: *Trio Sonata No. 1 in F*

7 Benjamin Britten: *Spring Symphony*

8 Wolfgang Amadeus Mozart: *String Quintet No. 4 in G minor*

Book choice *Shifts and Expedients of Camp Life* by William Barry Lord

Luxury choice A pair of binoculars

DAVID'S THIRD APPEARANCE 25 DECEMBER 1998
Music choices

1 Wolfgang Amadeus Mozart: 'Soave sia il vento' from *Cosi fan tutte*

2 George Frideric Handel: 'And the glory of the Lord' from *Messiah*

3 Johann Sebastian Bach: *Chromatic Fantasia and Fugue in D minor*

4 Duke Ellington & His Orchestra: 'Malletoba Spank'

5 Claudio Monteverdi: 'Zefiro torna' from *Scherzi musicali*

6 **Franz Schubert: *String Quintet in C major* – 2nd movement (favourite)**

7 William Walton: *Symphony No. 1 in B flat minor* – 2nd movement

8 Gustav Mahler: 'Ich bin der Welt abhanden gekommen' from *Rückert-Lieder*

Book choice *Shifts and Expedients of Camp* Life by William Barry Lord

Luxury choice A guitar

DAVID'S FOURTH APPEARANCE 29 JANUARY 2012
Music choices

1 Francisco Yglesia: 'Pajaro Campana' (The Bell Bird)

2 Franz Schubert: *Impromptu No. 1 in F minor Op. 142* – Sokolov

3 George Frideric Handel: 'And the Glory of the Lord' from *Messiah*

4 Clip: the superb lyre bird from *The Life of Birds*

5 **Johann Sebastian Bach: *3rd Goldberg Variation* (favourite)**

6 The Gamelan Orchestra: 'Legong'

7 Carl Michael Ziehrer: 'Wiener Burger, Walzer' (The New Year's Celebration from Vienna, 2012)

8 Wolfgang Amadeus Mozart: 'Soave sia il vento' from *Cosi fan tutte*

Book choice *Shifts and Expedients of Camp Life* by William Barry Lord

Luxury choice A piano

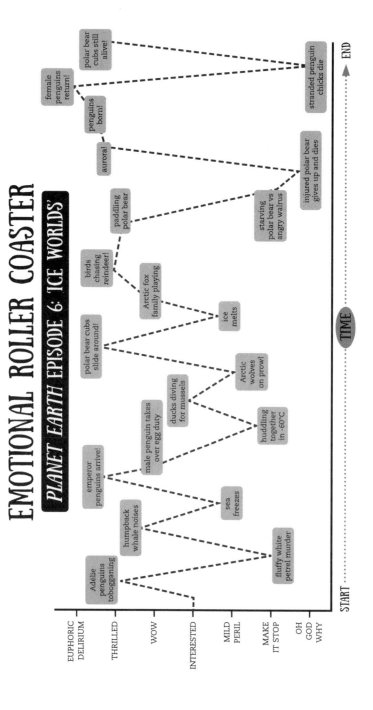

EMOTIONAL ROLLER COASTER

PLANET EARTH EPISODE 6: 'ICE WORLDS'

EUPHORIC
DELIRIUM

THRILLED

WOW

INTERESTED

MILD
PERIL

MAKE
IT STOP

OH
GOD
WHY

START .... TIME .... END

Adelie penguins tobogganing

humpback whale noises

fluffy white petrel murder

sea freezes

emperor penguins arrive!

male penguin takes over egg duty

huddling together in -60°C

ducks diving for mussels

Arctic wolves on prowl

polar bear cubs slide around!

ice melts

Arctic fox family playing

birds chasing reindeer!

paddling polar bear

starving polar bear vs angry walrus

injured polar bear gives up and dies

auroral

penguins born!

female penguins return!

polar bear cubs still alive!

stranded penguin chicks die

TWEETS POSTED WHILE WATCHING ATTENBOROUGH

Greg Jenner @greg_jenner
Mother Nature is an absolute d**k.
'Hi, welcome. You're alive. One
thing I should mention, KILLER
SNAKE ARMY. Good luck'
#PlanetEarth2

Dara Ó Briain
@daraobriain
Attenborough: Look at
this beautiful animal!
Us: Awwwww!
Attenborough: Now
watch it die, tragically,
and unloved!
#planetearth2

Thomas Gorton
@AngstromHoot
Attenborough has
no respect for crabs.
Always gives them
ridiculous music.
They are jesters to him

Alice @alicegregan
when u think uni is stressful
but then u watch #planetearth2
and realise u didn't have to
outrun racer snakes the day u
were born so alls gd

Liz Buckley @liz_buckley
I wish Blue Planet II wasn't
almost entirely made up of
things eating each other.
I thought there'd be more
recreational swimming.

TWITTER Q+A

On 6 January 2016, after just coming back from the Great Barrier Reef, Sir David agreed to answer questions on Twitter. Here is what we learned:

- His favourite British animal is a long-tailed tit.

- If he weren't a wildlife presenter, he would work in a museum.

- His least favourite creature is a rat.

- His favourite type of shark is a whale shark.

- His favourite reef fish is the humuhumunukunukuapua'a – a Hawaiian triggerfish.

- His hero growing up was Ernest Thompson Seton, an author and ranger on the prairies of California.

- If he could return as an animal, he'd be a sloth.

- If he could ask Charles Darwin anything, he'd ask why he thinks closely related species of oak, growing in similar ecologies, have different-shaped leaves.

- If he had to describe in one sentence the importance of nature for the human race it would be: 'We depend on the natural world for every mouthful of food we eat and every lungful of air we breathe.'

DAVID NARRATES YOU THROUGH BEING CAST AWAY ON A DESERT ISLAND

This male *Homo sapiens* takes his first steps alone on this desolate, unspoiled wilderness. Island life may look idyllic but he will be tested to the limit of human endurance.

His first challenge is to find a source of drinkable water. Rain or dew that has collected on obliging leaves may well save his life. No such luck, though, here. The water has already evaporated under the fierce sun.

He glances upwards at a nearby palm tree. The precious water within a coconut not only provides water but also potassium and sodium. The perfect remedy for a parched throat.

The only trouble is that they're twenty feet up.

Using his formidable brain, *Homo sapiens* fashions a rope by twisting the fibres from spent coconut husks. Wrapping the makeshift rope around his ankles provides the grip he needs to straddle the tree and shimmy upwards.

He twists the coconut stems until they come loose. Success! The battle is not won, though. He'll find that it's a tough nut to crack. He launches the coconut against the ridged trunk of the tree. This coconut will not yield without a fight, though.

Eventually his patience and persistence pay off and the first layer of defence is vanquished. He must now peel the husk

and find the seam that runs between the 'eyes' of the coconut. He strikes the seam with a good thwack. Nothing happens. He tries again but to no avail. To his relief, the nut cracks open at the third attempt.

Gulping down the lifeblood within, this extraordinary creature has bought himself at least a few days. He must now seek shelter.

DAVID NEVER UTTERS A CROSS WORD

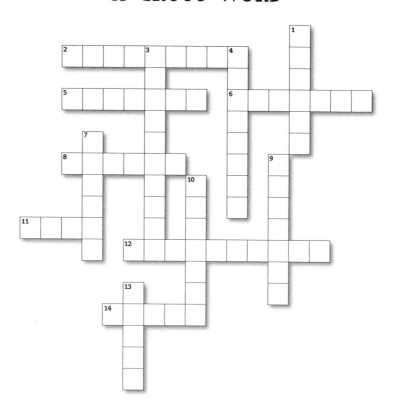

ACROSS

2 Longest venomous snake (two words)
5 Largest flightless bird
6 Deepest ocean trench
8 Largest cat in South America
11 Another name for the killer whale
12 Butterfly anagram: Real Madrid
14 Male bee

DOWN

1 Third biggest ocean
3 Shares 98.8 per cent of human DNA
4 Common fossil
7 Dog-like African predator
9 Largest penguin
10 Also called a sea cow
13 Whale food

PLANET EARTH II ENTIRE SERIES SCRIPT WORD CLOUD

almost
animals
away become birds
city comes creatures cub
danger desert earth feeding
feet female food forest grass
grasslands ground home hunt island
jungle land life leaves light male
miles million months living plants
mother mountains planet prey
world reach tree survive
water winter years
snow
soon
young
grow
rain

HONORARY DEGREES

Sir David has picked up a record 30 honorary degrees from British universities and three honorary fellowships. Oh, and a few international ones, as well …

BRITISH UNIVERSITIES

D.Litt., University of Leicester, 1970
D.Litt., City University, 1972
D.Litt., Birmingham University, 1972
D.Sc., University of Liverpool, 1974
Honorary Fellow, Manchester Polytechnic, 1976
LL.D. (Doctor of Law), University of Bristol, 1977
LL.D., University of Glasgow, 1977
D.Sc., Heriot-Watt University, 1978
D.Sc., University of Ulster, 1978
D.Sc., University of Sussex, 1978
D.Sc., University of Bath, 1978
D.Sc., Durham University, 1978
D.Sc., Keele University, 1978
D.Univ., Open University, 1980
Honorary Fellowship, Clare College, Cambridge, 1980
D.Sc., University of Cambridge, 1984
D.Sc., University of Oxford, 1988
D.Vet.Med., University of Edinburgh, 1994
D.Sc., Brunel University (London), 1995
D.Sc., University of Nottingham, 1999
D.Sc., Oxford Brookes University, 2003
D.Sc., University of the West of England, 2003
D.Univ., University of Roehampton, 2004
D.Sc., University of East Anglia, 2005
Honorary Fellowship, University of Leicester, 2007
D.Sc., University of Aberdeen, 2008
D.Sc., University of Exeter, 2008
D.Sc., Kingston University (London), 2008

D.Sc., Bangor University, 2009
D.Sc., Nottingham Trent University, 2010
D.Sc., University of Westminster, 2010
D.Sc., University of St Andrews, 2011
Queens University, Belfast, 2013 (for services to science and broadcasting)

INTERNATIONAL UNIVERSITIES

Antwerp University (Belgium), 1993
Ghent University (Belgium), 1997
University of Guelph (Canada), 2003
University of Iceland, 2006
Uppsala University (Sweden), 2007
Trinity College Dublin (Ireland), 2008
Nelson Mandela Metropolitan University (South Africa), 2010

WHERE'S DAVID?

Can you spot the world's most famous naturalist (in miniature) amid the foliage of the rainforest?

WIT & WISDOM FLIRTING

David's legendary flirting skills melted the heart of Cameron Diaz on *The Graham Norton Show* on 25 May 2012.

Cameron Diaz: *I did want to be a zoologist – that was what I thought I was going to be my entire life. I wanted to study the behaviour of animals.*

David Attenborough (leaning in very close to Cameron; audience laughter): *I could teach you all sorts of things.*

CD: *I've learned a lot from you already* (blushing). *A few things that I picked up backstage – I'm not going to mention those* (audience laughter). *But I ended up studying the behaviour of animals, it just happened to be human animals.*

DA: *Really?*

CD: *Yes, as an actor that's what I do, I study human behaviour.*

DA: *Lots of discoveries?*

CD: *Yes, lots of discoveries.*

DA: *Big surprises?*

CD: *Big surprises! I find so many more surprises when I watch your shows.*

DA: *Really?* (audience laughter) *You should see the outtakes!* (audience laughter)

CD: *I would love to see the outtakes! Maybe we can arrange a viewing.*

DA: *Yes, any time!*

EMOTIONAL ROLLER COASTER

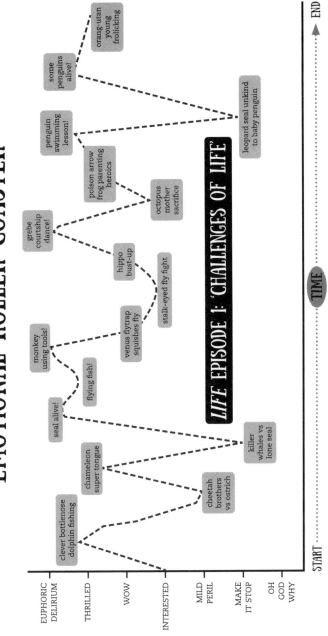

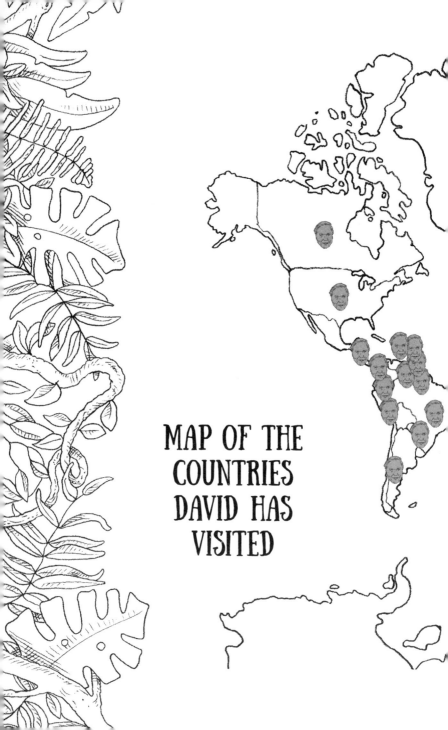

MAP OF THE
COUNTRIES
DAVID HAS
VISITED

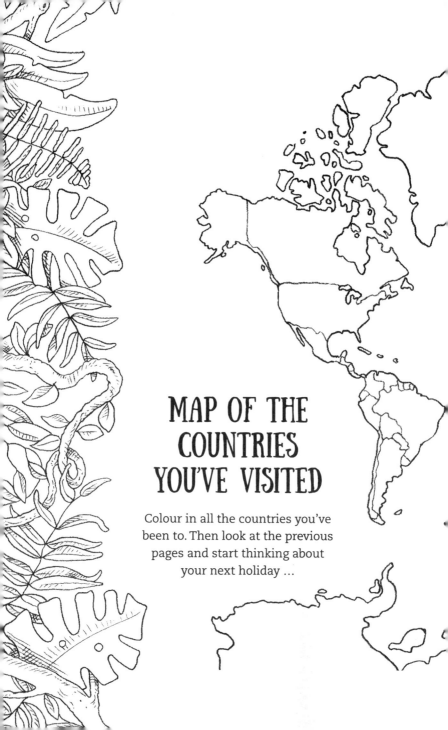

MAP OF THE COUNTRIES YOU'VE VISITED

Colour in all the countries you've been to. Then look at the previous pages and start thinking about your next holiday …

THE UK'S MOST-WATCHED PROGRAMMES OF 2017

Another gold medal for DA as *Blue Planet II* was named the best television programme of 2017 in a poll of TV critics. DA has the hearts and minds of critics and the general public. He should really be our leader.

And here are the top ten most-watched programmes of 2017. Guess who's at the top?

	PROGRAMME	DATE	VIEWERS (MILLIONS)
1	Blue Planet II	29 October	14.01
2	Strictly Come Dancing	16 December	13.01
3	I'm a Celebrity – Get Me Out Of Here!	9 November	12.21
4	Strictly Come Dancing: The Results	10 December	11.76
5	One Love Manchester	4 June	11.63
6	Sherlock	1 January	11.33
7	Broadchurch	17 April	11.21
8	Britain's Got Talent	6 May	10.94
9	Call The Midwife	19 February	10.63
10	New Year's Eve Fireworks	31 December	10.40

MATCH THE ANIMAL

MATCH THE ANIMAL TO ITS NEST

ANIMAL	NEST NAME
Seal	Sett
Ant	Lodge
Rabbit	Eyrie
Squirrel	Form
Otter	Nide
Beaver	Drey
Eagle	Warren
Badger	Formicary
Hare	Holt
Pheasant	Rookery

MATCH THE ANIMAL TO ITS ADJECTIVE

ANIMAL	ADJECTIVE
Otter	Vulpine
Snake	Aquiline
Crow	Ursine
Moth	Apian
Turtle	Equine
Bear	Lepidopterous
Fox	Lutrine
Horse	Corvine
Eagle	Serpentine
Bee	Chelonian

(Answers on page 187.)

CHARITY WORK

These are the charities and charitable trusts that David is involved with. Just in case you needed another reason to love him.

Amphibian Ark Initiative Patron
Australian Museum, Sydney Lifetime Patron
Blood Pressure Association Patron
British Dragonfly Society Patron
Butterfly Conservation President
Cool Earth (charity working against rainforest destruction) Supporter
The Conservation Volunteers Vice-President
Fauna & Flora International Vice-President
The Friends of Richmond Park Patron
The Grierson Trust (charity supporting documentary film-making) Patron
Lyme Regis Museum Patron
Population Matters (charity focusing on population size and its effects on environmental sustainability) Patron
Whitley Fund for Nature Trustee
The Wildfowl & Wetlands Trust Vice President
The Wildlife Trusts President Emeritus
World Land Trust Patron
WWF UK Ambassador (he was involved in the WWF from the beginning and served as one of their first trustees)

VIEWER CATCH-22

The same agony befalls all of us when we watch a David Attenborough documentary. He builds up our love for a cuddly creature. Then we see an equally cuddly creature. Cue formerly cuddly first creature ripping head off second creature. I hate you, Attenborough.

Here's how the drama tends to unfold. I'm using the Arctic fox mother vs snow goose chick example from *Planet Earth* episode 7: 'The Great Plains'.

1 CUTE ARCTIC FOX PLAYING IN HABITAT. POINT MADE BY DAVID THAT IT WILL STARVE IF IT DOESN'T GET FOOD SOON. (**Audience:** we love cuddly fox!)

2 EQUALLY CUTE BABY SNOW GOOSE PLAYING IN HABITAT. (**Audience:** we love sweet snow goose!)

3 SUDDEN PANIC! DANGER APPROACHING! (**Audience:** Oh God. Who are we rooting for?)

4 ARCTIC FOX TRANSFORMS FROM CUDDLY TOY TO VICIOUS MURDERER. (**Audience:** we hate formerly cuddly fox!)

5 ARCTIC FOX RETURNS TO FAMILY WITH FOOD. FAMILY SURVIVES. (**Audience:** we love fox!)

6 PARTING SHOT OF SNOW GOOSE MOTHER LOOKING FOR CHICK. (**Audience:** we hate fox!)

It's no wonder I've lost weight researching this book.

PUZZLE

Name all the films you can that have an animal in the title.

You've got two minutes!

(Answers on page 187.)

ATTENBOROUGH KARAOKE 'HERE COMES THE PRESENTER'

Here's my Attenborough-inspired remix of the first two verses and the chorus of Ini Kamoze's 1994 smash hit 'Here Comes the Hotstepper'.

Here comes the presenter, Attenborough
He's a national treasure, Attenborough
Picks up the viewers in de area, Attenborough
Love him just like that, Attenborough

No no he won't die, love for him multiplies
Anyone listening knows he's still the king
Attenborough knows (he knows)
He knows what you don't know
Pick up your litter and go, uh-oh!
Ch-ch-chang change (the world)

Here comes the presenter, Attenborough
He's a national treasure, Attenborough
Excuse me mister polluter, says Attenborough
Clean up your act, says Attenborough

WIT & WISDOM
CONSERVATION

'Ever since we arrived on this planet as a species, we've cut them down, dug them up, burnt them and poisoned them. Today we're doing so on a greater scale than ever.'

'Anyone who believes in indefinite growth on a physically finite planet is either mad or an economist.'

'The only way to save a rhinoceros is to save the environment in which it lives, because there's a mutual dependency between it and millions of other species of both animals and plants.'

'It seems to me that the natural world is the greatest source of excitement; the greatest source of visual beauty; the greatest source of intellectual interest. It is the greatest source of so much in life that makes life worth living.'

MAKE YOUR OWN ACROSTIC POEM

Compose your own little ditty in honour of David.

A _____

T _____

T _____

E _____

N _____

B _____

O _____

R _____

O _____

U _____

G _____

H _____

DAVID NARRATES YOU THROUGH BEING CAST AWAY ON A DESERT ISLAND

Desert islands can be surprisingly cold as night draws in.

This male *Homo sapiens* must build a shelter to help keep him warm and provide a barrier against the worst of the weather. Fortunately, this fallen tree will provide him with the roofline of a lean-to shelter. He collects smaller logs and places them at 45-degree angles either side of the tree.

With the framework established, he can now collect smaller branches and leaves to cover his shelter and block up the entrance. It's not much, but it's home for now.

With water and shelter secured, he must now find warmth.

He will find all the ingredients he needs on this island. These dry palm leaves and small twigs will do nicely for kindling, while bits of bark and dry grass will work well for tinder.

Next he must find a softwood branch, a few hardwood sticks and a sharp stone. He fashions a groove in the softwood with the stone and places the tinder inside. With as much vigour as he can muster, he rubs the hardwood stick up and down the groove to generate friction. It's not easy but, with determination, he'll get there.

On the verge of exhaustion, his persistence finally pays off.

He blows on the flame lightly and adds the dry grass and twigs, one by one. Soon he has a basic fire going, which will not only keep him warm, it will also ward off any predators, provide a flame for cooking and purifying water, and help to signal to any planes flying overhead.

Hope is kindled.

ATTENBOROUGH FIELD NOTES
EARLY BBC CAREER

- David was offered a job as an assistant producer and worked on the quiz show *Animal, Vegetable, Mineral?* (1952–59), choosing mystery objects that a panel of experts would try to identify.

- The first natural history programme David produced was *The Pattern of Animals*, a three-part series that aired in 1953. It examined why animals are shaped and patterned the way they are.

- In 1954, David and London Zoo's curator of reptiles, Jack Lester, came up with the programme *Zoo Quest*. Each episode involved footage of David and Jack's expedition to a tropical location to catch an animal for the zoo's collection. Towards the end of each series, the animals were introduced live in the studio, where an expert London Zoo panel would discuss them.

- The filming of the first episode of *Zoo Quest* began in September 1954. David, Jack Lester, cameraman Charles Lagus and Alf Woods, the head keeper of the bird house at London Zoo, travelled to Sierra Leone to try to find and capture (among other creatures) *Picathartes gymnocephalus* – a crow that few people had ever seen alive.

- The first *Zoo Quest* programme aired six weeks later. Jack presented the programme but was actually suffering from an unknown tropical disease. His condition worsened and he was taken to the Hospital for Tropical Medicine. Tragically, Jack died in 1956 after recurrences of the still-unidentified disease.

- The second *Zoo Quest* programme was already advertised in the *Radio Times*, but the team was without a presenter. Enter David Attenborough. Cyril Jackson, the departmental finance manager, summoned David to tell him: 'Just one thing about your studio appearance. It comes in a special category in my books called "Staff – No Fee".'

- *Zoo Quest* was the most successful wildlife programme of its time and continued for seven seasons, establishing David as a presenter.

- In 1956, David was working on the third series of *Zoo Quest*. While in Borneo, they heard of a hunter who had killed a female orangutan that had been eating his crops. The orangutan had a baby which the hunter kept in a wooden crate. David negotiated to exchange the team's remaining salt and tobacco for the infant orangutan, which they named Charlie. Charlie went on to father the first orangutan born at London Zoo!

MATCH THE ANIMAL

MATCH THE ANIMAL TO ITS COLLECTIVE NOUN

ANIMAL	COLLECTIVE NOUN
Apes	Intrusion
Bats	Cackle
Butterflies	Murmuration
Cockroaches	Prickle
Crocodiles	Shiver
Crows	Crash
Eagles	Bouquets
Ferrets	Skulk
Finches	Ostentation
Flamingoes	Bask
Foxes	Shrewdness
Grasshoppers	Kaleidoscope
Hyenas	Murder
Larks	Business
Locusts	Wake
Moles	Flamboyance
Owls	Cloud
Parrots	Maelstrom
Peacocks	Scream
Pheasants	Exaltation
Porcupines	Squabble
Ravens	Labour
Rhinos	Colony
Salamanders	Pandemonium
Seagulls	Descent
Sharks	Plague
Starlings	Parliament
Swifts	Unkindness
Vultures	Charm
Woodpeckers	Convocation

(Answers on page 187.)

SPECIES FACTFILE
DAVIDUS ATTENBOROUGHUS

HONORARY DEGREES FROM BRITISH UNIVERSITIES   30

SPECIES NAMED AFTER HIM 20 (plus 1 genus)

DOCUMENTARIES 115

POSTNOMINAL HONOURS 8

HIGHEST VIEWING FIGURES 14.01 MILLION*

LEAST FAVOURITE CREATURE RAT

FAVOURITE CHOCOLATE BAR CADBURY'S FRUIT & NUT**

AGE
92

BOOKS
WRITTEN
26

RANDOM FACT Only person in history
to have won BAFTAs for programmes in
black and white, colour, HD, 3D and 4K

* *Blue Planet* episode 1:
'One Ocean', 29 October 2017

** He's recently given up chocolate,
so don't send him a bar in the post

SPOT THE DIFFERENCE

Can you spot the seven differences between this rainforest scene and the one opposite?

(Answers on page 188.)

'An understanding of
the natural world and
what's in it is a source of
not only a great curiosity
but great fulfilment.'

FIND THE REAL SPECIES

Can you spot the real species lurking among this frankly ludicrous-sounding collection of animals?

1A Sarcastic Fringehead
1B Bombastic Curtainhead
1C Fantastic Fringehead

2A Tinseltassle
2B Sparklemuffin
2C Twinkleteacake

3A Strawberry Wandering Ant
3B Blueberry Meandering Ant
3C Raspberry Crazy Ant

4A Pink Fairy Armadillo
4B Yellow Unicorn Armadillo
4C Red Elf Armadillo

(Answers on page 188.)

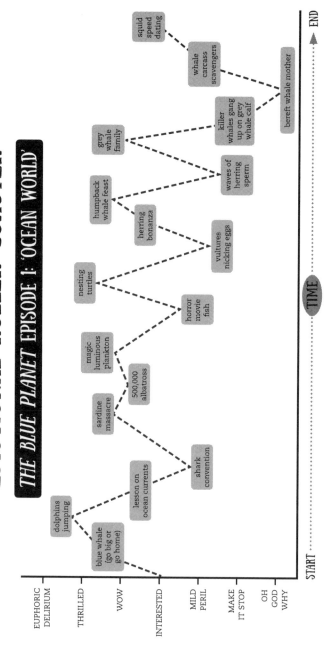

EMOTIONAL ROLLER COASTER

THE BLUE PLANET EPISODE 1: 'OCEAN WORLD'

EUPHORIC DELIRIUM
THRILLED
WOW
INTERESTED
MILD PERIL
MAKE IT STOP
OH GOD WHY

START
TIME
END

dolphins jumping
blue whale (go big or go home)
lesson on ocean currents
shark convention
sardine massacre
500,000 albatross
magic luminous plankton
horror movie fish
nesting turtles
vultures nicking eggs
herring bonanza
humpback whale feast
waves of herring sperm
grey whale family
killer whales gang up on grey whale calf
whale carcass scavengers
squid speed dating
bereft whale mother

FIND THE FOSSIL MAZE

Can you give the world's most famous naturalist a hand to guide him towards his beloved ammonite?

WHERE'S DAVID?

Can you spot the world's most famous naturalist (in miniature) amid the scrubland of the African savanna?

WIT & WISDOM
GLOBAL WARMING

'There is no question that climate change is happening; the only arguable point is what part humans are playing in it.'

'Many individuals are doing what they can. But real success can only come if there is a change in our societies and in our economics and in our politics.'

'We really need to kick the carbon habit and stop making our energy from burning things. Climate change is also really important. You can wreck one rainforest then move, drain one area of resources and move on to another, but climate change is global.'

'I would be absolutely astounded if population growth and industrialisation and all the stuff we are pumping into the atmosphere hadn't changed the climatic balance. Of course it has. There is no valid argument for denial.'

'I believe that if we find ways of generating and storing power from renewable resources, we will make the problem with oil and coal and other carbon fuels disappear because, economically, we will wish to use these other methods. And if we do that, a huge step will have been taken towards solving the problems of the Earth.'

PLANET EARTH II
FACTS IN NUMBERS

40 DIFFERENT COUNTRIES

89 MEMBERS OF THE CAMERA CREW

2,089 TOTAL SHOOTING DAYS

Planet Earth II is the first television series produced by the BBC in **4K** (ultra-high definition)

1 CAMERAMAN STUNG BY A **STINGRAY**

400 TERABYTES EQUIVALENT TO **82,000** DVDs of footage was recorded

- **FIRST-EVER** footage of the Araguaian river dolphin, only discovered in 2014

- **FIRST TIME** French catfish have been filmed feeding on town pigeons

- **FIRST-EVER** footage of peregrine falcons carrying out cooperative hunting sorties in an urban setting

- **FIRST-EVER** footage of a desert long-eared bat attacking a death stalker scorpion

- **FIRST TIME** lions have been shown hunting giraffes

- **FIRST TIME** racer snakes have been filmed hunting marine iguanas

- **'MOST COMPLETE'** film of snow leopard behaviour ever achieved

THE WORLD'S MOST TRAVELLED PERSON

David may well be the most travelled person alive or dead. During the filming of *Life of Birds* alone, he travelled 256,000 miles.

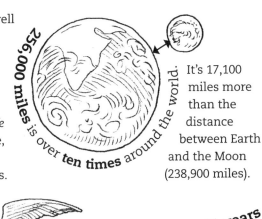

256,000 miles is over ten times around the world.

It's 17,100 miles more than the distance between Earth and the Moon (238,900 miles).

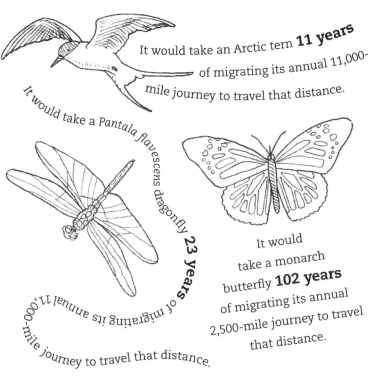

It would take an Arctic tern **11 years** of migrating its annual 11,000-mile journey to travel that distance.

It would take a Pantala flavescens dragonfly **23 years** of migrating its annual 11,000-mile journey to travel that distance.

It would take a monarch butterfly **102 years** of migrating its annual 2,500-mile journey to travel that distance.

CRITICALLY ENDANGERED MAMMALS

The 202 mammals below feature on the International Union for Conservation of Nature (IUCN) Red List of Threatened Species 2017 as 'Critically Endangered'.

Addax • African Wild Ass • Alaotra Reed Lemur • Andaman White-toothed Shrew • Angel Island Mouse • Armenian Whiskered Bat • Aru Flying Fox • Atlantic Humpbacked Dolphin • Bactrian Camel • Bala Tube-nosed Bat • Bavarian Pine Vole • Bawean Deer • Biak Giant Rat • Big Pocket Gopher • Black-and-white Ruffed Lemur • Black Bearded Saki • Black Crested Gibbon • Black-faced Lion Tamarin • Black Dorcopsis • Black Rhinoceros • Black-spotted Cuscus • Blonde Capuchin • Blond Titi Monkey • Blue-eyed Black Lemur • Blue-eyed Spotted Cuscus • Bolivian Chinchilla Rat • Bornean Banded Langur Monkey • Bornean Orangutan • Bouvier's Red Colobus Monkey • Brown-headed Spider Monkey • Buff-headed Capuchin • Bulmer's Fruit Bat • Caquetá Tití Monkey • Carpentarian Rock-rat • Cao-vit Gibbon • Catalina Deer Mouse • Celebes Crested Macaque • Central Rock-rat • Chalchalero Viscacha Rat • Chiapan Climbing Rat • Chinanteco Deer Mouse • Chinese Pangolin • Christmas Island Shrew • Claire's Mouse Lemur • Colombian Woolly Monkey • Coronados Deer Mouse • Cotton-headed Tamarin • Cozumel Harvest Mouse • Dama Gazelle • Delacour's Langur Monkey • De Winton's Golden Mole • Diademed Sifaka • Dickey's Deermouse • Dryas Monke • Dwarf Hutia • Eastern Gorilla • Ecuadorian White-fronted Capuchin • Eisentraut's Mouse Shrew • Emma's Giant Rat • Emperor Rat • Ethiopian Amphibious Rat • European Mink • Fijian Monkey-faced Bat • Fleurete's Sportive Lemur • Gerp's Mouse Lemur • Gilbert's Potoroo • Gloomy Tube-nosed Bat • Golden Bamboo Lemur • Golden-crowned Sifaka • Golden-mantled Tree Kangaroo • Golden Vizcacha Rat • Greater Bamboo Lemur • Greater Monkey-faced Bat • Grey-shanked Douc Langur Monkey • Guadalcanal Rat • Hainan Gibbon • Handley's Slender Mouse Opossum • Harenna Shrew • Heavenly Hill Rat • Hill's Horseshoe Bat • Hirola • Indri • Ixtlán Deer Mouse • Jamaican Flower Bat • Jamaican Greater Funnel-eared Bat • James' Sportive Lemur • Javan Rhinoceros • Javan Slow Loris • Jenkin's Shrew • Kipunji • Large-antlered Muntjac Deer • Lord Howe Long-eared Bat • Ka'apor Capuchin • Kolar Leaf-nosed Bat • Kondana Rat • Kouprey • Lamotte's Roundleaf Bat • Large Rock-rat • Leadbeater's Possum • Little Earth Hutia • Livingstone's Flying Fox • *Lophuromys eisentrauti* • Malabar Civet

• Manusela Mosaic-tailed Rat • Mantiqueira Atlantic Tree Rat • Marohita Mouse Lemur • Mayan Deer Mouse • Mexican Agouti • Miss Waldron's Red Colobus Monkey • Mongoose Lemur • Montserrat Island Deermouse • Montane Monkey-faced Bat • Mountain Pygmy Possum • Mount Kahuzi Climbing Mouse • Mount Oku Hylomyscus • Myanmar Snub-nosed Monkey • Namdapha Flying Squirrel • Nelson's Small-eared Shrew • Nelson's Woodrat • New Caledonia Long-eared Bat • New Zealand Greater Short-tailed Bat • Nicobar Shrew • Niger Delta Red Colobus Monkey • Northern Glider • Northern Hairy-nosed Wombat • Northern Idaho Ground Squirrel • Northern Muriqui • Northern White-cheeked Gibbon • Nosy Be Sportive Lemur • Okinawa Spiny Rat • Pacific Dagu • Pagai Island Macaque • Perote Deer Mouse • Perrier's Sifaka • Peruvian Yellow-tailed Woolly Monkey • Philippine Bare-backed Fruit Bat • Phillips' Congo Shrew • Pig-tailed Snub-nosed Monkey • Poncelet's Giant Rat • Preuss's Red Colobus • Puebla Deer Mouse • Pygmy Hog • Pygmy Raccoon • Pygmy Three-toed Sloth • Red Crested Tree Rat • Red Ruffed Lemur • Red Wolf • Reig's Tuco-tuco • Riverine Rabbit • Roig's Tuco-tuco • Rondo Dwarf Galago • Sahafary Sportive Lemur • Sahamalaza Peninsula Sportive Lemur • Saiga • San Cristobal Shrew • San Esteban Deermouse • San Jose Brush Rabbit • San Lorenzo Deermouse • San Martin Titi Monkey • San Quintin Kangaroo Rat • Santa Catarina's Guinea Pig • Saola • Sclater's Shrew • Schmidly's Deer Mouse • Seychelles Sheath-tailed Bat • Siau Island Tarsier • Sibree's Dwarf Lemur • Silky Sifaka (large white lemur) • Single-striped Opossum • Sir David's Long-beaked Echidna • Slender-tailed Deer Mouse • Social Tuco-tuco • Sumatran Orangutan • Sumatran Rhinoceros • Sunda Pangolin • Talaud Bear Cuscus • Tamaraw • Tapanuli Orangutan • Telefomin Cuscus • Tenkile • Thomas's Big-eared Bat • Thongaree's Disc-nosed Bat • Tonkin Snub-nosed Monkey • Tropical Pocket Gopher • Tumbalá Climbing Rat • Unicolored Tree Rat • Vancouver Island Marmot • Vaquita • Vanikoro Flying Fox • Variegated Spider Monkey • Visayan Warty Pig • Western Gorilla • Western Long-beaked Echidna • Western Ringtail Possum • White-collared Lemur • Wimmer's Shrew • Woylie • Wondiwoi Tree-kangaroo • Yanbaru Whiskered Bat • Yangtze River Dolphin • Zuniga's Dark Rice Rat

MATCH THE ANIMAL

MATCH THE BABY ANIMAL NAME TO THE ANIMAL

ANIMAL	BABY ANIMAL NAME
Alligator	Poult
Antelope	Squab
Bat	Infant
Cicada	Kid
Deer	Kit
Dove	Cheeper
Ferret	Hatchling
Goat	Kitten
Goose	Baby
Gorilla	Foal
Hare	Puggle
Horse	Gosling
Kangaroo	Cygnet
Lemur	Fawn
Oyster	Pup
Partridge	Calf
Platypus	Joey
Rabbit	Nymph
Swan	Spat
Turkey	Leveret

(Answers on page 188.)

ATTENBINGO

The perfect way to get competitive while watching an Attenborough documentary! Cross out the boxes when each one of the following occurs:

DAVID APPEARS!	CREATURE JUST MAKES IT OUT ALIVE!	CREATURE LOOKS LIKE IT'S GOING TO MAKE IT OUT ALIVE BUT GETS SAVAGELY TORN APART	EMOTIONAL MUSIC AS FAMILY GET A MEAL ONCE MORE
YOU FEEL THE HORRIBLE CONFLICT BETWEEN BEING HAPPY FOR THE FAMILY THAT GET TO AVOID STARVATION AND SAD FOR THE EX-ANIMAL	DRAMATIC WEATHER EVENT	HEARTFELT MESSAGE ABOUT CONSERVATION	FEEL THE SENSE OF AWKWARDNESS AS TWO ANIMALS ENGAGE IN AN ACT OF INTIMACY AND YOU REMEMBER YOU'RE WATCHING WITH YOUR PARENTS
DAVID GETS EXCITED!	CUTE CREATURE PLAYING JOYFULLY, UNAWARE OF INEVITABLE TRIAL TO FOLLOW	PENGUIN WALK!	CREATURE LEARNS HOW TO USE TOOLS
SLIGHTLY DRY PART OF EPISODE ABOUT OCEAN CURRENTS, FUNGI OR MOSS	YOU WORK OUT THE ANSWER TO THE QUESTION: WHAT PATRONUS WOULD DAVID CAST?	THE LAST LINE IN THE SCRIPT BEFORE THE BIT ABOUT HOW THE TEAM FILMED IT	BABY ANIMAL FALLS OVER, A BIT LIKE BAMBI

GUESS THE ANIMALS

Can you guess the animals David's talking about?

1 *'The Kalahari's most cantankerous resident. They don't like company. And they certainly don't like sharing a water hole with lions.'*

A African Wild Dog
B Black Rhinoceros
C Common Hippo
D Cape Buffalo

2 *'Its tube-like body has to stretch so extremely to accommodate such a gigantic meal that its flanks have torn.'*

A Boa Constrictor
B Western Terrestrial Garter Snake
C African Rock Python
D King Cobra

3 *'Having your body encased in shell obviously brings problems and one of them is how do you mate? Making love in a suit of armour is not easy.'*

A Galapagos Tortoise
B Long-tailed Pangolin
C Caribbean Hermit Crab
D Garden Snail

4 *'Just in case his call is inaudible he makes his message clear with a wave. And his rival waves back. He repeats his message so there's no misunderstanding.'*

A American Bullfrog
B Large Brown Mantis
C Asian Shield Mantis
D Panamanian Golden Frog

5 'They're superb acrobats, adapted to leaping from trunk to trunk. But where the gap is too great or in more open stretches of river bank, they abandon the trees and do something extraordinary. Their hind legs are too long to walk on all fours. So they stay upright and gallop.'

A Black-headed Spider Monkey

B Sifaka

C Proboscis Monkey

D Ring-tailed Lemur

6 'Those two discs on its face channel sound into its two ears, which are on a slightly different level on the head, and that difference enables the bird to pinpoint the source of the sound, whether it's in the air, or down on the ground.'

A Barn Owl

B Hen Harrier

C Atlantic Puffin

D Great Grey Owl

7 'It now spends most of its time above the ground, marching its way through the undergrowth, where it feeds on tree-sap and fallen fruit. This hefty powerful creature may not look as if it could fly. But it can.'

A Giant Burrowing Cockroach

B Saint Helena Earwig

C Madagascar Hissing Cockroach

D Atlas Beetle

8 'Having a beak longer than your body does have its drawbacks. For a start, it's tricky to keep it clean.'

A Common Toucan

B Rhinoceros Hornbill

C Sword-billed Hummingbird

D Roseate Spoonbill

(Answers on page 189.)

SPOT THE DIFFERENCE

Can you spot the seven differences between this savanna scene and the one opposite?

(Answers on page 189.)

CRITICALLY ENDANGERED BIRDS

The 222 birds below feature on the IUCN Red List of Threatened Species 2017 as 'Critically Endangered'.

Akekee • Alagoas Antwren • Alagoas Foliage-gleaner • Alagoas Tyrannulet • Amsterdam Albatross • Annobon Scops-owl • Antioquia Brush-finch • Araripe Manakin • Bachman's Warbler • Baer's Pochard • Bahama Oriole • Balearic Shearwater • Bali Myna • Beck's Petrel • Belem Curassow Bengal Florican • Black-breasted Puffleg • Black-chinned Monarch • Black-faced Honeycreeper • Black-hooded Coucal • Black Stilt • Black-winged Myna • Black-winged Trumpeter • Blue-bearded Helmetcrest • Blue-billed Curassow • Blue-crowned Laughingthrush • Blue-eyed Ground-dove • Blue-fronted Lorikeet • Blue-throated Macaw • Bugun Liocichla • Brazilian Merganser • Bryan's Shearwater • California Condor • Cebu Brown-dove • Cebu Flowerpecker • Cerulean Paradise-flycatcher • Chatham Shag • Cherry-throated Tanager • Chestnut-capped Piha • Chilean Woodstar • Chinese Crested Tern • Christmas Frigatebird • Cozumel Thrasher • Crested Honeycreeper • Crested Shelduck • Crow Honeyeater • Cryptic Treehunter • Cuban Kite • Djibouti Francolin • Dwarf Ibis • Edwards's Pheasant • Eskimo Curlew • Fatu Hiva Monarch • Fiji Petrel • Flores Hawk-eagle • Galapagos Petrel • Giant Ibis • Glaucous Macaw • Glittering Starfrontlet • Golden White-eye • Gorgeted Puffleg • Gough Finch • Great Indian Bustard • Grenada Dove • Grey-backed Myna • Grey-rumped Myna • Guadalupe Storm-petrel • Guanacaste Hummingbird • Helmeted Hornbill • Himalayan Quail • Hoary-throated Spinetail • Hooded Grebe • Hooded Vulture • Horned Curassow • Imperial Woodpecker • Indian Vulture • Indigo-winged Parrot • Iphis Monarch • Isabela Oriole • Ivory-billed Woodpecker • Jamaican Petrel • Jamaican Poorwill • Javan Blue-banded Kingfisher • Javan Green Magpie • Javan Lapwing • Javan Pied Starling • Jerdon's Courser • Juan Fernandez Firecrown • Junin Grebe • Kakapo • Kauai Creeper • Kauai Nukupuu • Kinglet Calyptura • Laysan Duck • Lendu Crombec • Liben Lark • Long-billed Forest-warbler • Madagascar Fish-eagle • Madagascar Pochard • Magenta Petrel • Makira Moorhen • Malherbe's Parakeet • Mangrove Finch • Maranon Spinetail • Mariana Crow • Marquesas Kingfisher • Marsh Antwren • Masafuera Rayadito • Mascarene Petrel • Maui Akepa • Maui Nukupuu • Maui Parrotbill • Mauritius Olive White-eye • Medium Tree-finch • Millerbird • Mindoro

Bleeding-heart Pigeon
• Moorea Reed-warbler
• Munchique Wood-wren
• Negros Bleeding-heart
Pigeon • Negros Fruit-dove •
New Caledonian Buttonquail •
New Caledonian Lorikeet •
New Caledonian Nightjar • New
Caledonian Owlet-nightjar • New Caledonian Rail • New Zealand
Storm-petrel • Newton's Fiscal • Nias Hill Myna • Niceforo's Wren •
Nihoa Finch • Northern Bald Ibis • Oahu Creeper • Okinawa Woodpecker
• Olomao • Orange-bellied Antwren • Orange-bellied Parrot • Ou • Palila •
Pernambuco Pygmy-owl • Philippine Cockatoo • Philippine Eagle • Pink-
headed Duck • Plains-wanderer • Pohnpei Starling • Polynesian Ground-dove
• Poo-Uli • Principe Thrush • Puerto Rican Parrot • Purple-winged Ground-
dove • Raso Lark • Red-headed Vulture • Red-throated Lorikeet • Regent
Honeyeater • Reunion Cuckooshrike • Ridgway's Hawk • Rimatara Reed-
warbler • Rio Branco Antbird • Rota White-eye • Royal Cinclodes • Rück's
Blue-flycatcher • Rufous-fronted Laughingthrush • Rufous-headed Hornbill •
Rüppell's Vulture • Saipan Reed-warbler • Samoan Moorhen • Sangihe Dwarf-
kingfisher • Sangihe Golden Bulbul • Sangihe Whistler • Sangihe White-eye
• Santa Marta Wren • Sao Tome Grosbeak • Sapphire-bellied Hummingbird •
Semper's Warbler • Seychelles Paradise-flycatcher • Short-crested Coquette
• Siau Scops-owl • Siberian Crane • Silvery Pigeon • Sinu Parakeet • Sira
Curassow • Slender-billed Curlew • Slender-billed Vulture • Small Kauai
Thrush • Sociable Lapwing • Socorro Mockingbird • South Island Kokako
• Southern Red-breasted Plover • Spix's Macaw • Spoon-billed Sandpiper
• Stresemann's Bristlefront • Sulu Bleeding-heart Pigeon • Sulu Hornbill
• Sulu Racquet-tail • Sumatran Ground-cuckoo • Swift Parrot • Tachira
Antpitta • Tahiti Monarch • Taita Apalis • Taita Thrush • Tooth-billed Pigeon •
Townsend's Shearwater • Trinidad Piping-guan • Tristan Albatross • Tuamotu
Kingfisher • Turquoise-throated Puffleg • Ua Pou Monarch • Ultramarine
Lorikeet • Urrao Antpitta • Waved Albatross • White-backed Vulture •
White-bellied Cinclodes • White-bellied Heron • White-chested White-eye
• White-eyed River Martin • White-headed Vulture • White-rumped Vulture
• White-shouldered Ibis • White-winged Flufftail • White-winged Guan •
Yellow-breasted Bunting • Yellow-crested Cockatoo • Zapata Rail

DAVID NARRATES YOU THROUGH BEING CAST AWAY ON A DESERT ISLAND

The male *Homo sapiens* gazes out across the expanse of blue in front of him. Water, water, everywhere, but not a drop to drink.

Despite successfully fashioning a harness to climb a palm tree, he is running out of coconuts. This human must find a reliable fresh water supply. A man will survive for several weeks without food, but after three days without water his body will suffer dramatically.

Not a drop of rain has fallen since he washed ashore. The situation looks bleak.

He does, however, have a clear waterproof anorak. In the city, this jacket will shield him from a light shower. On this desert island, this jacket can prove to be the difference between life and death. It works as a makeshift distillation device, transforming impure water into fresh water. He will just need to find a cup-like receptacle and fill it with salty water. This coconut shell will do nicely.

First he must dig a hole and place the receptacle at the bottom. The jacket needs to cover the hole and so the edges need to be weighed down using stones. The centre of the jacket also needs to be weighed down to form a funnel.

The process is simple. The sun shines through the plastic layer, heating the impure water until it begins to evaporate. Clean water vapour travels upwards and condenses into water on the underside of the plastic. After a few hours, this sun-parched human will quench his thirst and will live another day.

WHERE'S DAVID?

Can you spot the world's most
famous naturalist (in miniature)
amid this desert scene?

EMOTIONAL ROLLER COASTER

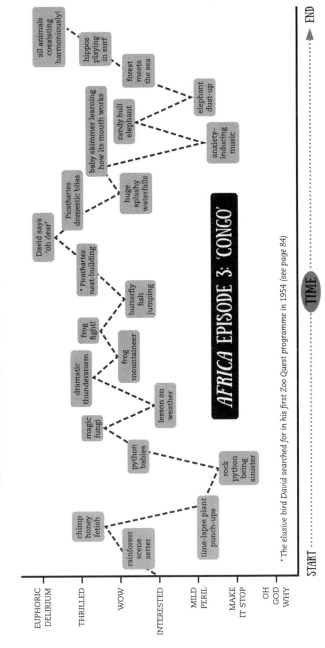

AFRICA EPISODE 3: 'CONGO'

* The elusive bird David searched for in his first Zoo Quest programme in 1954 (see page 84)

EUPHORIC DELIRIUM
THRILLED
WOW
INTERESTED
MILD PERIL
MAKE IT STOP
OH GOD WHY

START ......

TIME

END

all animals coexisting harmoniously!
hippos playing in surf
forest meets the sea
elephant dust-up
baby skimmer learning how its mouth works
randy bull elephant
anxiety-inducing music
Picathartes domestic bliss
huge splashy waterfalls
David says 'oh dear'
Picathartes nest-building
butterfly fish jumping
frog fight!
frog mountaineer
dramatic thunderstorm
lesson on weather
magic fungi
python babies
rock python being sinister
chimp honey fetish
rainforest scene setter
time-lapse plant punch-ups

WIT & WISDOM GOD

'I often get letters, quite frequently, from people who say how they like the programmes a lot, but I never give credit to the almighty power that created nature. To which I reply and say, "Well, it's funny that the people, when they say that this is evidence of the Almighty, always quote beautiful things. They always quote orchids and hummingbirds and butterflies and roses." But I always have to think too of a little boy sitting on the banks of a river in West Africa who has a worm boring through his eyeball, turning him blind before he's five years old. And I reply and say, "Well, presumably the God you speak about created the worm as well," and now, I find that baffling to credit a merciful God with that action. And therefore it seems to me safer to show things that I know to be truth, truthful and factual, and allow people to make up their own minds about the moralities of this thing, or indeed the theology of this thing.'

from the BBC documentary *Life on Air*, 2002

'As far as I'm concerned, if there is a supreme being then He chose organic evolution as a way of bringing into existence the natural world ... which doesn't seem to me to be necessarily blasphemous at all.'

'I don't think an understanding and an acceptance of the four-billion-year-long history of life is any way inconsistent with a belief in a supreme being ... And I am not so confident as to say that I am an atheist.'

MATCH THE ANIMAL

MATCH THE BABY ANIMAL NAME TO THE ANIMAL

ANIMAL	BABY ANIMAL NAME
Butterfly	Piglet
Camel	Infant
Cat	Maggot
Cheetah	Spiderling
Donkey	Peachick
Fly	Calf
Goat	Kitten
Grasshopper	Fingerling
Hawk	Foal
Hedgehog	Joey
Heron	Tadpole
Llama	Nymph
Mole	Chick
Monkey	Cub
Peafowl	Kid
Skunk	Caterpillar
Spider	Cria
Toad	Kit
Trout	Pup
Wallaby	Eyas

(Answers on page 189.)

WAR ON PLASTIC

The most powerful message of *Blue Planet II* was the disastrous effect of single-use plastic on marine life. David's rallying cry had an immediate effect, with Buckingham Palace declaring a war on plastic, the BBC unveiling plans to ban single-use plastic from 2020 and Sky investing £25 million to address the plastic crisis.

A NORMAL PLASTIC BOTTLE TAKES ABOUT **450** YEARS TO BREAK DOWN COMPLETELY

BETWEEN **4** AND **12** MILLION METRIC TONNES OF PLASTIC ENDS UP IN THE OCEAN EACH YEAR

AN ESTIMATED **270,000** TONNES OF PLASTIC IS FLOATING ON THE OCEAN'S SURFACE

As of 2015, around **8.3 billion tonnes** of plastic waste had been generated

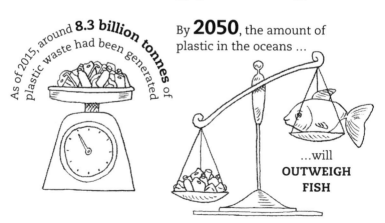

By **2050**, the amount of plastic in the oceans …

…will **OUTWEIGH FISH**

Some estimates suggest that up to **100,000** marine mammals accidentally consume plastic debris each year

PLASTIC POLLUTION AFFECTS AT LEAST **700** MARINE SPECIES

HERE ARE SEVERAL THINGS YOU CAN DO:

TAKE A REUSABLE BOTTLE OR COFFEE CUP WITH YOU

BRING YOUR OWN CUTLERY RATHER THAN TAKE THE FREE PLASTIC ONES

AVOID PRODUCTS WITH **PLASTIC PACKAGING**. BUYING LOOSE FRUIT AND VEGETABLES IS BETTER FOR THE ENVIRONMENT AND CHEAPER!

CARRY REUSABLE SHOPPING BAGS

DON'T USE PLASTIC STRAWS. GO FOR PAPER ONES OR BRING A REUSABLE ONE

FIND THE REAL SPECIES

Can you spot the real species lurking among this frankly ludicrous-sounding collection of animals?

1A Lollipop Worms
1B Ice Cream Cone Worms
1C Sherbet Worms

2A Odd-tailed Tyrant
2B Strange-tailed Tyrant
2C Tassel-tailed Tyrant

3A Fried Egg Jellyfish
3B Scrambled Egg Jellyfish
3C Confit Egg Jellyfish

4A Pacific Spined Lumpfish
4B Pacific Spiky Lumplicker
4C Pacific Spiny Lumpsucker

(Answers on page 189.)

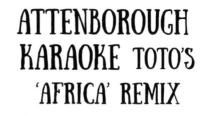

ATTENBOROUGH KARAOKE TOTO'S 'AFRICA' REMIX

OK, with a few tweaks, this feels like it could be Attenborough's anthem. A couple of the lines I haven't even needed to change!

I hear the show is on tonight
Heartfelt whispers about conservation
Sir David, our shining light
A living legend and a viewing sensation
He'll guide you along the way
On a journey through long forgotten lands and ancient seas
He turns to us as if to say, 'Hurry chaps, it's waiting there for you'

When he leaves us, what the hell are we gonna do?
He's done more than a hundred men or more could ever do
We've seen the rains down in Africa
He's shown us things we never knew we had

The wild dogs cry out in the night
As they grow restless, longing for his company
I know that we must do what's right
As sure as Kilimanjaro rises like Olympus above the Serengeti
We need to save the creatures outside; they're frightened of what
    we've become

When he leaves us, what the hell are we gonna do?
He's done more than a hundred men or more could ever do
We've seen the rains down in Africa
Gonna take some time to do the things we never had

Hurry guys, he's waiting there for you!

THE QUEEN AND I

So he's not only the king of the jungle and television royalty, but he's also a real royal (sort of), if you trace his family tree far enough back!

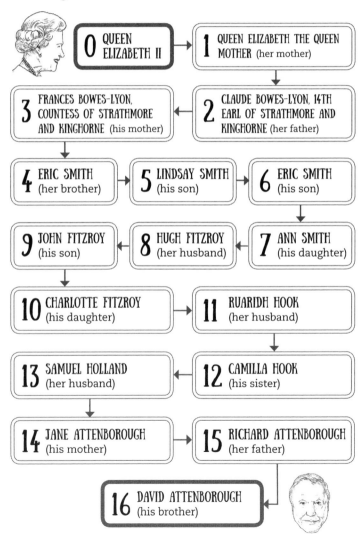

0 QUEEN ELIZABETH II

1 QUEEN ELIZABETH THE QUEEN MOTHER (her mother)

3 FRANCES BOWES-LYON, COUNTESS OF STRATHMORE AND KINGHORNE (his mother)

2 CLAUDE BOWES-LYON, 14TH EARL OF STRATHMORE AND KINGHORNE (her father)

4 ERIC SMITH (her brother)

5 LINDSAY SMITH (his son)

6 ERIC SMITH (his son)

9 JOHN FITZROY (his son)

8 HUGH FITZROY (her husband)

7 ANN SMITH (his daughter)

10 CHARLOTTE FITZROY (his daughter)

11 RUARIDH HOOK (her husband)

13 SAMUEL HOLLAND (her husband)

12 CAMILLA HOOK (his sister)

14 JANE ATTENBOROUGH (his mother)

15 RICHARD ATTENBOROUGH (her father)

16 DAVID ATTENBOROUGH (his brother)

DRAW DAVID ON THE £20 NOTE

The new £20 note will be issued in 2020. Replacing the Scottish economist Adam Smith on the back of the note will be the painter J.M.W. Turner. 'Travesty,' I hear you cry! And you wouldn't be alone, seeing as the country's top choice in a poll of 2,128 people conducted by YouGov in October 2017 was none other than our Sir David. Here's a chance to right the wrong by designing your own David Attenborough-themed £20 note.

Twenty Pounds £20

£H

KA34 517771

Bank of England

KA34 517771

DAVID ATTENBOROUGH 1926 –

KA34 517771

ATTENBOROUGH FIELD NOTES
BBC CAREER

- In 1962, David returned to university to study social anthropology at the London School of Economics. The BBC agreed to let David work as a freelance providing them with programme ideas.

- BBC2's launch night in April 1964 was a disaster, with a fire at Battersea Power Station causing a power failure. The public and press were not impressed by the new channel's editorial direction, so the BBC's Controller of Programmes, Huw Weldon, offered David the job. He accepted and became Controller of BBC2 in March 1965, under the proviso that he could continue to make a programme of his choosing every 18 months.

- David commissioned a wave of new programmes including *Chronicle* and *Horizon*. He even helped develop the one-day cricket format and a rugby league competition played under floodlights, called the BBC2 Floodlit Trophy. He also booked appearances by great American jazz and swing greats including Duke Ellington, Louis Armstrong and Ella Fitzgerald.

- In 1967, the government told the BBC that they could introduce colour television. David oversaw the change, and the first programme to be shot in colour was the nightly interview programme *Late Night Line-Up*.

Novelist Anthony Burgess was one of the guests. However, the first live colour broadcast was the tennis at Wimbledon on 1 July 1967.

- David decided the channel needed a new symbol and musical sting to indicate to viewers watching in black and white that they were transmitting in colour. Picasso was invited to draw the symbol and Stravinsky to write the music. Picasso suggested a colour television set instead of a fee. However, Picasso would only agree to drawing the symbol if Stravinsky agreed to write the music, but the latter died two weeks later.

- David was in charge of preparing a schedule of exciting programmes to encourage viewers to pay £5 for the colour licence fee. He commissioned the hugely successful documentary series *Civilisation*, written and presented by former Director of the National Gallery Sir Kenneth Clark.

- Despite the success of *Civilisation*, David was criticised by Aubrey Singer, the BBC's Head of Science Programmes, who was outraged that a man of science would commission an arts subject for such prestigious treatment. And so David commissioned the 13-part documentary series *The Ascent of Man*, written and presented by mathematician Jacob Bronowski.

- In 1969, David was also responsible for commissioning the now legendary *Monty Python's Flying Circus* and snooker tournament *Pot Black*, which was credited with popularising the sport.

ATTENBOROUGH WORDSEARCH

ATTENBOROUGH AND TV

```
T  T  G  A  L  A  P  A  G  O  S  I  A  Z  Q
O  H  E  A  L  P  G  T  M  M  B  F  B  O  O
L  W  E  N  V  I  X  Y  I  Y  R  G  F  O  W
T  R  N  L  A  B  F  I  X  I  K  R  C  Q  I
R  Y  M  K  I  L  Z  E  C  L  O  T  N  U  A
I  K  X  Y  H  V  P  A  O  Z  F  L  C  E  W
A  N  Y  X  T  Y  I  E  E  N  Y  R  R  S  U
L  F  U  Z  N  F  E  N  U  Q  A  L  Y  T  V
S  I  R  R  A  L  P  D  G  L  Q  I  G  X  J
O  Z  A  L  C  L  Q  B  Q  P  B  J  R  V  T
F  H  T  R  A  E  T  E  N  A  L  P  Y  K  Z
L  U  H  N  L  X  A  J  W  P  U  A  R  L  N
I  J  E  E  E  J  Z  V  R  Q  C  U  N  Y  O
F  T  L  S  O  L  G  V  E  J  U  O  J  E  X
E  E  T  A  C  R  A  Z  K  Q  C  E  S  Z  T
```

AFRICA   GALAPAGOS
FROZEN PLANET   THE LIVING PLANET
PLANET EARTH   COELACANTH
ZOO QUEST   LIFE ON AIR
BLUE PLANET   TRIALS OF LIFE

(Answers on page 189.)

WRITE DOWN ALL THE ANIMAL SPECIES YOU SEE THIS WEEK

WHERE'S DAVID?

Can you spot the world's
most famous naturalist
(in miniature) amid
this polar scene?

EMOTIONAL ROLLER COASTER

LIFE EPISODE 5: 'BIRDS'

START .... TIME .... ▶ END

EUPHORIC
DELIRIUM

THRILLED

WOW

INTERESTED

MILD
PERIL

MAKE
IT STOP

OH
GOD
WHY

- spatule-tailed hummingbird!
- vultures smashing bones
- bearded vultures soaring
- one tropicbird makes it through!
- tropicbird parent robbed by frigate bird
- red knot feeding frenzy
- nesting flamingo colony
- chinstrap penguins riding waves
- penguin rush hour
- pelicans swallowing baby gannets
- grebe water dance
- sage grouse wobble board
- displaying birds of paradise
- bowerbird collecting red objects
- rejected by female!
- first bowerbird gets lucky
- flamingo promenade

ATTENBOROUGH HIP-HOP ALBUM COVERS

So here's what would have happened if David had released LL Cool J's 1989 album *Walk Like a Panther*.

DAVID NEVER UTTERS A CROSS WORD

ACROSS

2 The national animal of New Zealand

4 February 2nd is the traditional date that this fabled species of rodent emerges from its burrow

8 IUCN Red List category between 'Near Threatened' and 'Endangered'

9 Which country's flag features a yellow bird of paradise?

12 David's home town and favourite place in the world

13 American national bird

14 David's middle name

DOWN

1 Country in which David famously played with a mountain gorilla family

3 Something a long-suffering coyote might chase; also the state bird of New Mexico

5 Island home of the world's largest tortoises

6 Environmental organisation founded in 1969

7 The ring-tailed lemur is a resident of this unique island

10 The UK's only poisonous snake

11 Darwin's famous ship

EXTINCT ANIMALS

The 362 animals below feature on the IUCN Red List of Threatened Species 2017 as 'Extinct'.

ACTINOPTERYGII (RAY-FINNED FISHES)

Ameca Shiner • Amistad Gambusia • *Anabarilius macrolepis* • *Aplocheilichthys* sp. nov. 'Naivasha' • Ash Meadows Poolfish • *Barbus microbarbis* • Beyşehir Bleak • Blackfin Cisco • Charco Azul Pupfish • *Chondrostoma scodrense* • Clear Lake Splittail • *Coregonus bezola* • *Coregonus fera* • *Coregonus gutturosus* • *Coregonus hiemalis* • *Coregonus restrictus* • *Ctenochromis pectoralis* • *Cyprinus yilongensis* • Danube Delta Gudgeon • Deepwater Cisco • Durango Shiner • Eğirdir Minnow • *Evarra bustamantei* • *Evarra eignemanni* • *Evarra tlahuacensis* • Gölçük Toothcarp • Graceful Priapella • Gravenche • Harelip Sucker • Houting • Hula Bream • Iznik Shemayav • Las Vegas Dace • Longjaw Cisco • Long Jaw Tristramella • Maryland Darter • New Zealand Grayling • Pahranagat Spinedace • *Pantanodon madagascariensis* • Parras Characodon • Parras Pupfish • Perritos De Sandia • Phantom Shiner • *Ptychochromis onilahy* • Salado Shiner • *Salmo pallaryi* • *Salvelinus neocomensis* • *Salvelinus profundus* • San Marcos Gambusia • Santa Cruz Pupfish • Scioto Madtom • Siamese Flat-barbelled Catfish • Silver Trout • Snake River Sucker • Stumptooth Minnow • Techirghiol Stickleback • *Telestes ukliva* • Thicktail Chub • *Tristramella intermedia* • *Tristramella magdelainae* • Utah Lake Sculpin • Villa Lopez Pupfish • Whiteline Topminnow • *Xystichromis bayoni*

AMPHIBIANS

Ainsworth's Salamander • *Atelopus vogli* • Eungella Gastric-brooding Frog • Golden Toad • Gunther's Streamlined Frog • Heredia Robber Frog • Kelaart's Starry Shrub Frog • Las Vegas Leopard Frog • Longnose Harlequin Frog • McCranie's Robber Frog • Mount Glorious Torrent Frog • *Pseudophilautus adspersus* • *Pseudophilautus dimbullae* • *Pseudophilautus eximius* • *Pseudophilautus extirpo* • *Pseudophilautus halyi* • *Pseudophilautus leucorhinus* • *Pseudophilautus maia* • *Pseudophilautus malcolmsmithi* • *Pseudophilautus nanus* • *Pseudophilautus oxyrhynchus* • *Pseudophilautus pardus* • *Pseudophilautus rugatus* • *Pseudophilautus stellatus* • *Pseudophilautus temporalis* • *Pseudophilautus zal* • Quito Stubfoot Toad • Rumassala Shrub Frog • Sharp-snout Pygmy Treefrog • Southern Gastric Brooding Frog • Spiny-knee Leaf Frog • Variable Bush Frog • Webless Shrub Frog • Yunnan Lake Newt

BIRDS

Aguijan Reed-warbler • Alaotra Grebe • Aldabra Brush-warbler • Amaui • Amsterdam Duck • Ascension Crake • Atitlan Grebe • Auckland Merganser • Bar-winged Rail • Bermuda Flicker • Bermuda Hawk • Bermuda Night-heron • Bermuda Saw-whet Owl • Bermuda Towhee • Bishop's Oo • Black-fronted Parakeet • Black Mamo • Bonin Grosbeak • Bonin Thrush • Bonin Woodpigeon • Brace's Emerald • Broad-billed Parrot • Bridled White-eye • Bushwren • Canarian Oystercatcher • Caribbean (or Gould's) Emerald • Carolina Parakeet • Chatham Bellbird • Chatham Fernbird • Chatham Rail • Choiseul Pigeon • Christmas Sandpiper • Colombian Grebe • Cuban Macaw • Dieffenbach's Rail • Dodo • Eiao Monarch • Finsch's Duck • Forster's Reed-warbler • Grand Cayman Thrush • Great Auk • Greater Amakihi • Greater Koa-finch • Guadalupe Caracara • Guadeloupe Parakeet • Guadeloupe Parrot • Guam Flycatcher • Guam Reed-warbler • Hawaii Akialoa • Hawaii Mamo • Hawaii Oo • Hawaiian Rail • Hawkins's Rail • Hodgen's Waterhen • Huia • Kakawahie • Kangaroo Island Emu • Kauai Oo • Kauai Akialoa • King Island Emu • Kioea • Kona Grosbeak • Kosrae Crake • Kosrae Starling • Mangareva Reed-warbler • Labrador Duck • Lanai Akialoa • Lanai Hookbill • Large Kaua'i Thrush • Large St Helena Petrel • Laughing Owl • Laysan Honeycreeper • Laysan Rail • Least Vermilion Flycatcher • Lesser

Koa-finch • Liverpool Pigeon • Lord Howe Gerygone • Maupiti Monarch • Marquesan Swamphen • Marianne White-eye • Martinique Amazon • Mascarene Coot • Mascarene Parrot • Mauritius Blue-pigeon • Mauritius Duck • Mauritius Grey Parrot • Mauritius Night-heron • Mauritius Owl • Mauritius Shelduck • Mauritius Turtle-dove • Mauritius Woodpigeon • Miller's Rail • Moorea Sandpiper • Mysterious Starling • New Caledonia Gallinule • New Zealand Little Bittern • New Zealand Quail • Norfolk Kaka • Norfolk Starling • North Island Piopio • North Island Snipe • North Island Takahe • Nuku Hiva Monarch • Oahu Akepa • Oahu Akialoa • Oahu Nukupuu • Oahu Oo • Oceanic Parrot • Pagan Reed-warbler • Paradise Parrot • Passenger Pigeon • Raiatea Parakeet • Raiatea Starling • Red-moustached Fruit-dove • Red Rail • Réunion Fody • Réunion Gallinule • Réunion Ibis • Réunion Kestrel • Réunion Night-heron • Réunion Owl • Réunion Pigeon • Réunion Rail • Réunion Shelduck • Réunion Starling • Robust White-eye • Rodrigues Blue-pigeon • Rodrigues Night-heron • Rodrigues Owl • Rodrigues Parakeet • Rodrigues Parrot • Rodrigues Rail • Rodrigues Solitaire • Rodrigues Starling • Rodrigues Turtle-dove • Ryukyu Woodpigeon • Seychelles Parakeet • Slender-billed Grackle • Small St Helena Petrel • Snail-eating Coua • South Island Piopio • South Island Snipe • Spectacled Cormorant • Stephens Island Rockwren • St Helena Crake • St Helena Cuckoo • St Helena Hoopoe • St Helena Rail • Tahiti Rail • Tahiti Sandpiper • Tanna Ground-dove • Thick-billed Ground-dove • Tristan Moorhen • Ula-ai-hawane • Wake Rail • White Swamphen •

CEPHALASPIDOMORPHS (JAWLESS FISHES) *Eudontomyzon* sp. nov. 'migratory'

MAMMALS *Atalaye Nesophontes* • Aurochs • Big-eared Hopping-mouse • Bluebuck • Blue-grey Mouse • Bramble Cay mosaic-tailed rat • Broad-cheeked Hopping-mouse • Broad-faced Potoroo • Buhler's Coryphomys • Bulldog Rat • Candango Mouse • Capricorn Rabbit-rat • Caribbean Monk Seal • Christmas Island Pipistrelle Bat • Crescent Nailtail Wallaby • Cuban Coney • Darling Downs Hopping-mouse • Darwin's Galapagos Mouse • Desert Bandicoot • Desert Bettong • Desert Rat Kangaroo • *Dusicyon avus* • Eastern Hare-wallaby • Edith's Island-shrew • Falklands Wolf • Galápagos Giant Rat • Giant Fossa • Gould's Mouse • Greater Cuban Nesophontes • Guam Flying Fox • Haitian Nesophontes • Hispaniolan Edible Rat • Imposter Hutia • Indefatigable Galapagos Mouse • Indo-chinese Warty Pig • Insular Cave Rat • Jamaican Monkey • Jamaican Rice Rat • Japanese Sea Lion • *Lagostomus crassus* • Lake Mackay Hare-wallaby • Large Palau Flying Fox • Large Sloth Lemur • Lesser Rabbit-eared Bandicoot • Lesser Mascarene Flying-fox • Lesser Stick-nest Rat • Little Swan Island Hutia • Long-eared Mouse • Long-tailed Hopping-mouse • Maclear's Rat • Madagascan Dwarf Hippopotamus • Marcano's Solenodon • Martinique Muskrat • Montane Hutia • Nelson's Rice Rat • Nevis Rice Rat • Nullarbor Dwarf Bettong • Oriente Cave Rat • Pemberton's Deer Mouse • Percy Island Flying Fox • Pig-footed Bandicoot • Puerto Rican Hutia • Queen of Sheba's Gazelle • Red-bellied Gracile Mouse Opossum • Saint Lucia Giant Rice Rat • Samana Hutia • Sardinian Pika • Saudi Gazelle • Schomburgk's Deer • Sea Mink • Short-tailed Hopping-mouse • Steller's Sea Cow • St Michel Nesophontes • St Vincent Pygmy Rice Rat • Tasmanian Tiger • Toolache Wallaby • Torre's Cave Rat • Vespucci's Rodent • Western Cuban Nesophontes • White-footed Rabbit-rat

REPTILES Barbados Racer • Cape Verde Giant Skink • Christmas Island Whiptail-skink • *Contomastix charrua* • Delcourt's Sticky-toed Gecko • Domed Mauritius Giant Tortoise • Domed Rodrigues Tortoise • Floreana Giant Tortoise • Guadeloupe Ameiva • Günther's Dwarf Burrowing Skink • Hoffstetter's Worm Snake • *Leiocephalus cuneus* • *Leiolopisma mauritiana* • Martinique Curlytail Lizard • Navassa Curlytail Lizard • Navassa Rhinoceros Iguana • Pinta Giant Tortoise • Redonda Skink • Reunion Giant Tortoise • Rodrigues Giant Day Gecko • Round Island Burrowing Boa • Saddle-backed Mauritius Giant Tortoise • Saddle-backed Rodrigues Giant Tortoise • Saint Lucia Skink • Seychelles Mud Turtle • Tonga Ground Skink • Underwood's Mussurana

DRAW SIR DAVID'S SUPERHERO ALTER EGO

Now I know he's a superhero already, but the blue linen shirt and khaki trouser combo won't sell comics. We're after a suitable costume and a suitable superhero name. If you're stuck, drawing Captain Planet with David's face is perfectly acceptable.

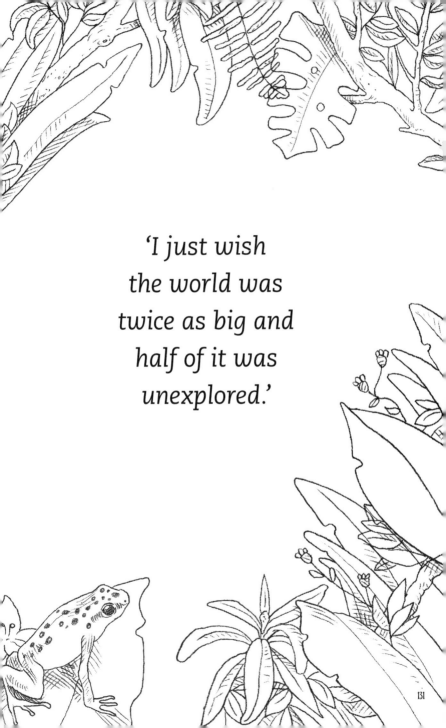

'I just wish
the world was
twice as big and
half of it was
unexplored.'

ANIMAL ANAGRAMS

Can you unscramble the following words to find the animals?

TOAST ....

TORTE ....

TUTOR ....

GREET ....

MANIAC ....

LOO ETC ....

STOREY ....

SKELTER..................................

SEAL WE ....

SOOT CUP ....

AROLED ....

BALANCER ....

UNFOLDER ....

GIRLS TAN ....

STRAYING ....

QUITS MOO ....

NEAT TEAR ....

HEATS PAN ....

RAPTOR .... BRISK PONG ....

TEACH HE .... PLANE TOE ....

THRONE .... LONG PAIN ....

ORCA CON .... TAILOR LAG ....

EMANATE .... RADIO MALL ....

SANDIER .... OLIVE WREN ....

EMITTER .... OSCAR WAYS ....

CHAINED .... CARROT NOM ....

LEG LAZE .... UPPER COIN ....

TRASH ME .... DREAMS ALAN ....

FEAR FIG .... IMPEACH ZEN ....

(Answers on page 189–190.)

WIT & WISDOM HUMANITY

'I think sometimes we need to take a step back and just remember we have no greater right to be here than any other animal.'

'The one creature that really makes my jaw sag, that I find absolutely fascinating so much that I can hardly stop looking at it, is a nine-month-old human baby.'

'I suspect that happiness is not a state but rather a transition. If things are getting better, and circumstances. You'll find people where their conditions aren't changing in any way, it's rather rare for them to be happy. And you get that bubbling happiness when you achieve things.'

'The fact is that no species has ever had such wholesale control over everything on Earth, living or dead, as we now have. That lies upon us, whether we like it or not, an awesome responsibility. In our hands now lies not only our own future, but that of all other living creatures with whom we share the Earth.'

ATTENBOGGLE

How many words can you find on the Boggle board below?
Only words of four or more letters please!

(Answers on page 190.)

ANIMAL MISHAPS

ELEPHANT SEAL

'This is a beach master and there are a dozen or so like him spaced out along this beach. Each one of them has his own harem and I estimate that this one has about a hundred females in his. And his sole object in life at the moment is to make sure that he and he alone mates with every single one of them. And to that end he must fight.'

(Randy elephant seal turns on our hero, who defends himself with a walking stick.)

MALE CAPERCAILLIE

'He is so charged up, this being the breeding season, that he will display to almost anything, including me!'

(David knocked over by aforementioned randy capercaillie.)

GREATER BIRD OF PARADISE

Take 1 David: This surely … (CUT due to bird squawking)

Take 2 David: This surely is one … (CUT due to bird squawking)

Take 3 Close up, the plumes are truly exquisite … (CUT due to bird squawking)

Take 4 Of course, by the eighteenth century, naturalists realised that birds of paradise did have legs. Even so … (CUT due to bird squawking)

Take 5 By about the eighteenth century. Very well. (CUT due to bird squawking)

Take 6 But Carl Linnaeus, the great classifier of the natural world, when he came to allocate a scientific name to this bird, called it (bird makes WOOHOO noise) woohoo! (David laughs) *Paradisia apoda* – the bird of paradise without legs.

BLUE PLANET II FACTS IN NUMBERS

39 DIFFERENT COUNTRIES

6,000 TOTAL SHOOTING HOURS

1,000 SHOOTING HOURS IN SUBMERSIBLES

4 YEARS TO FILM AND PRODUCE

125 SHOOTS

10 HOURS The time crewmembers spent in a submersible without being able to GO TO THE TOILET

Only 3 people have gone deeper than the *Blue Planet II* team: DON WALSH and JACQUES PICCARD (oceanographers who went to Challenger Deep, the deepest point on the Earth's seabed in 1960), and film director JAMES CAMERON in 2012

5 babies WERE BORN TO CREWMEMBERS during the filming

1 NEW SPECIES DISCOVERED: the ethereal snailfish, which was the deepest-living fish ever found, until the mariana snailfish was discovered in December 2017

The **ETHEREAL SNAILFISH** can withstand pressure equivalent to the weight of **50 JUMBO JETS** stacked on top of each other

DESIGN YOUR OWN ATTENBOROUGH TATTOOS

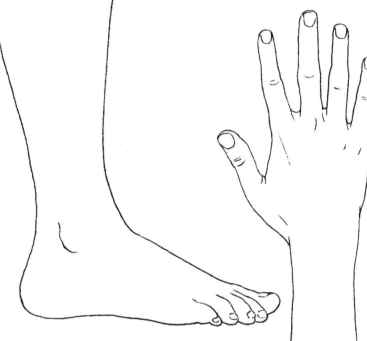

Some people's dedication to the great man goes far beyond my humble offerings. In April 2016, Samantha Ordish from Hampshire got a huge tattoo of Sir David on her arm in a scene featuring a gorilla, two hummingbirds, a golden-headed lion tamarin, two red-eyed tree frogs, and a keel-billed toucan. And in May 2016, super-fan Matt Daly from Jersey got an equally huge tattoo of Sir David on his leg to commemorate the legendary broadcaster's 90th birthday. Here's your chance to design your own Sir David-themed tattoos.

ATTENBOROUGH FIELD NOTES
RETURN TO BROADCASTING

- In 1969, David was made the BBC's Director of Programmes with a seat on the Board of Management. He viewed the prospect 'with some dismay' because it would take him another step away from making programmes. He resigned four years later to return to programme making.

- David's first natural history series after resigning from the BBC was the six-part *Eastwards with Attenborough* (1973), highlighting little-known parts of Indonesia.

- The first big wildlife series David wrote and presented was *Life on Earth*, which was partly funded by Warner Brothers. While negotiations were taking place for this hugely ambitious project, David wrote and presented *The Tribal Eye* (1975), about tribal art, and *The Explorers* (1975), about famous explorers including Cook, Amundsen and Columbus.

- *Life on Earth* was a 13-part series that took three years to make and aired in January 1979. It featured David's legendary encounter with a group of mountain gorillas in Rwanda, who groomed and played with him. *Life on Earth* was sold to 100 territories and watched by approximately 500 million people worldwide, establishing David as a cultural icon.

- However, the US TV network that had inherited the series cited that David's accent could not be understood in various parts of the US. They wanted to cut the scenes of David talking to the camera and replace the narration with the voice of Robert Redford. David's contract terms meant that he had to give approval but he refused. Eventually, America's Public Broadcasting System bought the series and transmitted it. David's accent was perfectly comprehensible in all parts of the US.

- David's next major series was *The Living Planet*, which focused on how animals adapt to the environments they inhabit. It comprised 12 parts, first airing in January 1984, and took nearly four years to make. It was another major international success for the BBC.

- David was in London in November 1981 on a break from filming. He was attending one of his first meetings as one of the British Museum's trustees, surrounded by dukes and ambassadors, but left rather suddenly. He had been passed a note by one of the museum's messengers, before asking the chairman: 'May I have permission to leave? I have to film a volcano that has just started to erupt in Iceland.' *The Living Planet* team left for Heathrow immediately.

CRITICALLY ENDANGERED REPTILES

The 266 reptiles below feature on the IUCN Red List of Threatened Species 2017 as 'Critically Endangered'.

Acanthodactylus harranensis • *Acanthodactylus mechriguensis* • Aeolian Wall Lizard • Agalta Mountain Forest Snake • Albany Adder • Alcatrazes Lancehead • Allan's Lerista • Ambre Forest Stub-Tailed Chameleon • Anatolian Mountain Steppe Viper • Anegada Skink • Antanosy Day Gecko • Andasibe Big-headed Snake • Anegada Rock Iguana • Ankafina Ground Snake • Annobon Lidless Skink • Antiguan Racer • Antioquia Swamp Lizard • Atlántida Dwarf Brown Snake • Antsiranana Blind Legless Skink • Arakan Forest Turtle • Asian Narrow-headed Softshell Turtle • Atalaye Curlytail Lizard • Atlantic Ridley Sea Turtle • Bami Toad-headed Agama • Barbados Leaf-toed Gecko • Barbados Skink • Barbados Threadsnake • Be'er Sheva Fringe-fingered Lizard • Belalanda Chameleon • Bermuda Skink • Bizarre-nosed Chameleon • Blue-tailed Galliwasp • Bog Turtle • Bojer's Skink • Boo-Liat's Kukri Snake • Bourret's Box Turtle • Bouvier's Leaf-toed Gecko • Brazilian Woodland Racer • Burmese Starred Tortoise • California Mountain Kingsnake • *Calumma tarzan* • Cap-Haitien Least Gecko • Carrot Rock Skink • Casuhatien Anole • Cayemite Short-tailed Amphisbaena • Cayman Brac Blindsnake • Cebu Small Worm Skink • Central American River Turtle • Central Haitian Curlytail • Chapman's Pygmy Chameleon • Charnali Lizard • Chinese Alligator • Chinese Three-striped Box Turtle • Clarion Racer • *Cnemaspis anaikattiensis* • Cochran's Least Gecko • Conception Bank Silver Boa • Cranwell's Tree Iguana • Cuban Crocodile • Cuban Khaki Trope • Culebra Giant Anole • Culebra Skink • Dahl's Toad-headed Turtle • Darevsky's Viper • Doumergue's Fringe-fingered Lizard • Durban Dwarf Burrowing Skink • Eastern Santa Cruz Giant Tortoise • Ebner's Skink • El Hierro Giant Lizard • *Emmochliophis miops* • Española Giant Tortoise • 'Eua Forest Gecko • *Euspondylus monsfumus* • Fernandina Giant Tortoise • Fiji Crested Iguana • Flat-tailed Tortoise • Flattened Musk Turtle • Frost's Arboreal Alligator Lizard • Galapagos Pink Land Iguana • Geometric Tortoise • Gharial • Giant Hispaniolan Galliwasp • Golden Lancehead • *Gonatodes infernalis* • Gonave Worm Lizard • Greater Martinique Skink • Greater Saint Croix Skink • Grenadines Clawed Gecko • Guanaja Long-tailed snake • Gulbaru Leaf-tailed gecko • Greater Virgin Islands Skink • Haensch's Whorltail Iguana • Haitian Border Threadsnake • Haitian Striped Sphaero • Harran Fringe-toed Lizard • Hawksbill Turtle • *Hemidactylus dracaenacolus* • Hispaniolan Four-lined Skink • Hispaniolan Tailspot Sphaero • Hispaniolan Ten-lined Skink • Hispaniolan Two-lined Skink • Hoge's Side-necked Turtle • *Homonota rupicola* • *Homonota taragui* • Honduran Red-banded Earth Snake • Hong Kong Blindsnake • Horton's Mabuya • Hoshell's Forest Racer • Indochinese Box Turtle • Isla Todos Santos Mountain Kingsnake • Jamaica Giant Galliwasp • Jamaican Iguana • Jamaican Racer • Jeypore Ground Gecko • Kaala Striped Gecko • Kemp's Ridley • Kigom Hills Worm Lizard • *Kinyongia mulyai* • Kikuzato's Stream Snake • Kleinmann's Tortoise • Koniambo Striped Gecko • Kopéto Smooth Skink • Knuckles Pygmy Lizard • Kopéto Elf Skink • Kunda Half-Toed Gecko • Lacépède's Ground Snake • Lancelin Island Skink • La Gomera Giant Lizard • La Hotte Blindsnake • La Palma Giant Lizard • Lapierre Curlytail Lizard • La Vega Racer • Leaf-scaled Sea Snake • Lesser Martinique Skink • Lesser

Saint Croix Skink • Lesser Virgin Islands Skink • Lima Leaf-toed Gecko • *Liolaemus aparicioi* • *Liolaemus azarai* • *Liolaemus curis* • *Liolaemus cuyumhue* • *Liolaemus paulinae* • Madagascar Big-headed Turtle • Madras Spotted Skink • Magdalena River Turtle • Magdalena Scaly-eyed Gecko • Marbled Gecko • Marche Leon Least Gecko • Mariana Skink • Marbled Day Gecko • Marie-Galante Skink • Masohoala Day Gecko • McCord's Box Turtle • Meier's Skink • Merendón Mountains Snaileater • *Mitophis asbolepis* • Mona Skink • Monito Skink • Montserrat Galliwasp • Montserrat Skink • Morne Dubois Least Gecko • Mountain Centipede Snake • Mount Francais Leaf-toed Gecko • Mount Kaala Marble-throated Skink • Mount Inago Pygmy Chameleon • Mount Namuli Pygmy Chameleon • Mount Taom Marble-throated Skink • Namoroka Leaf Chameleon • Neiba Agave Sphaero • Nevin's Slider • Nguru Spiny Pygmy Chameleon • Northern Dwarf Skink • Northern River Terrapin • Nubian Flapshell Turtle • Oaxaca Spiny-tailed Iguana • Okoloma Worm Lizard • Ono-i-Lau Ground Skink • Orinoco Crocodile • Orlov's Viper • Ornate Ground Snake • Ornate Shovel-snout • Paevala Nimble Gecko • Painted Terrapin • Palawan Forest Turtle • Pan's Box Turtle • Parish's Fanged Snake • Pestel Amphisbaena • Peters' Ameiva • Peters' Black-headed Snake • Philippine Crocodile • *Phrynocephalus horvathi* • *Phyllodactylus sommeri* • Pindai Dwarf Skink • Ploughshare Tortoise • Poum Striped Gecko • Prakke's Reed Snake • Pulau Tioman Ground Snake • Queretaro Desert Spiny Lizard • Rabino's Tree Iguana • Radiated Tortoise • Red-crowned Roofed Turtle • Redonda Ameiva • Reyes' Caribbean Gecko • *Rhampholeon hattinghi* • *Riama rhodogaster* • Ricord's Rock Iguana • Roatan Coral Snake • Roatán Skink • Ross' Wolf Snake • Rothschild's Skink • Roti Island Snake-necked Turtle • Saint Croix Racer • Saint Lucian Whiptail • Saint Martin Skink • Sakalava Legless Skink • Sakalava Short-legged Sand Skink • Salamanca Rock Lizard • Salt Marsh Gecko • Samana Least Gecko • Samana Threadsnake • Santa Catalina Island Rattlesnake • Santiago Giant Tortoise • Short-nosed Sea Snake • Siamese Crocodile • Sierra Curlytail Lizard • Slender-snouted Crocodile • Slender Limbless Slider • *Sombrero Ameiva* • Southern Even-fingered Gecko • Southern River Terrapin • Southern Viet Nam Box Turtle • Spider Tortoise • Striped Gecko • St Vincent Blacksnake • Sulawesi Forest Turtle • *Synophis plectovertebralis* • Tajikistan Even-fingered Gecko • Taom Striped Gecko • Tenerife Speckled Lizard • TerreNueve Least Gecko • Three-banded Centipede Snake • Tioman Reed Snake • Toyama's Ground Gecko • Transcaucasian Racerunner • Tsiafajavona dwarf gecko • Tunisian fringe-fingered Lizard • Turks and Caicos Rock Iguana • Turks Islands Skink • Turquoise Dwarf Gecko • Typical Madagascar Blind Snake • Utila Spiny-tailed Iguana • Vietnamese Pond Turtle • Virgin Islands Bronze Skink • Viquez's Tropical Ground Snake • Wagner's Viper • Western Chameleon Gecko • Western Santa Cruz Giant Tortoise • Western Swamp Turtle • Yamashina's Ground Gecko • Yangtze Giant Softshell Turtle • Yellow-headed Box Turtle • Yellow-lipped Grass Anole • Yoro Mountain Forest Snake • Yunnan Box Turtle • Zhou's Box Turtle • Zong's Odd-scaled Snake

DON'T DISAPPOINT DAVID

Cut this page out and hold it up in a variety of everyday situations, like if you're a parent and your troublesome teenager has caused you grief. Or if you want to complain about poor customer service at easyJet.

BLUE PLANET II
ENTIRE SERIES SCRIPT
WORD CLOUD

almost
animals around
blue changing chick coast
coral crab creatures
deep dolphins eggs feed female
fish food forests giant home hundreds
hunting life live male marine mate
metres miles numbers ocean
reef sea sharks
something start surface thousands
turtles waters whale
world years
young

'EXTINCT IN THE WILD' ANIMALS

The 71 animals and plants below feature on the IUCN Red List of Threatened Species 2017 as 'Extinct in the Wild'.

Alagoas Curassow (bird) • *Aylacostoma chloroticum* (snail) • *Aylacostoma guaraniticum* (snail) • *Aylacostoma stigmaticum* (snail) • *Betula szaferi* (plant of the birch family) • Black Softshell Turtle • Blue Cycad • Borrachero (plant) • *Bromus bromoideus* (true grass) • *Bromus interruptus* (true grass) • *Brugmansia aurea* (flowering plant) • *Brugmansia insignis* (flowering plant) • *Brugmansia sanguinea* (flowering plant) • *Brugmansia suaveolens* (flowering plant) • *Brugmansia versicolor* (flowering plant) • *Brugmansia vulcanicola* (flowering plant) • Butterfly Splitfin (bony fish) • Captain Cook's Bean Snail • Catarina Pupfish • Christmas Island Blue-tailed Shinning-skink • Christmas Island Chained Gecko • *Corypha taliera* (species of palm tree) • *Cyanea pinnatifida* (flowering plant) • *Encephalartos relictus* (South African seed plant) • *Erythroxylum echinodendron* (Cuban flowering plant) • Escarpment Cycad • *Euphorbia mayurnathanii* (Indian flowering plant) • *Firmiana major* (Chinese flowering plant) • Franklin Tree • Fuzzyflower Cyrtandra (Hawaiian plant) • Golden Skiffia (species of splitfin fish) • Governor Laffan's Fern • Guam Kingfisher • Guam Rail (flightless bird) • Hawaiian Crow • Inconnu (freshwater fish) • Kalimantan Mango • Kihansi Spray Toad • Lago Yojoa Palm • La Palma Pupfish • *Lysimachia minoricensis* (plant in the primula family) • *Mangifera rubropetala* (flowering plant) • Molokai Koki`o (small deciduous tree) • Moorean Viviparous Tree Snail (four species) • *Nymphaea thermarum* (water lily) • Oahu Deceptor Bush Cricket • Père David's Deer • Polynesian Tree Snail (five species) • Potosi Pupfish • *Rhododendron kanehirai* • Rose-tipped Partula Snail • Scimitar-horned Oryx (antelope) • *Senecio leucopeplus* (plant of daisy family) • She Cabbage Tree • Socorro Dove • Socorro Isopod (crustacean) • St Helena Redwood • Superb Cyanea (flowering plant) • *Terminalia acuminata* (tree) • Toromiro (flowering tree) • Wood's Cycad • Wyoming Toad

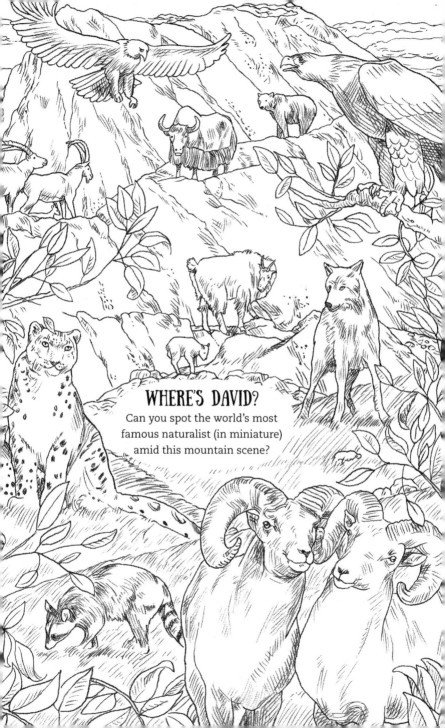

WHERE'S DAVID?

Can you spot the world's most
famous naturalist (in miniature)
amid this mountain scene?

ATTENBOROUGH FIELD NOTES
THE 1980s AND 1990s

- After the success of *The Living Planet*, David wanted a series illustrating complex behaviour patterns across the whole range of the animal kingdom. And so the 12-part *Trials of Life* series went into production, with each episode focusing on a major stage of life that animals have to undergo.

- The whole series took over three and a half years to film and David himself travelled over 250,000 miles during the filming.

- Multiple iconic moments occurred during the shoots. For the first time, chimpanzees were shown hunting colobus monkeys in a team; killer whales were filmed hunting sea lions on beaches in Patagonia; and millions of female Christmas Island red crabs were filmed on their annual march from the island's forests down to the sea.

- *The Sunday Telegraph* television critic A.N. Wilson wrote a review of *Trials of Life* exposing what he believed was behind-the-scenes trickery involving a male mallee fowl protecting his nest. Wilson said the encounter was 'almost certainly faked up with a shot of the bird kicking and another of Sir David getting sand in his eyes (probably thrown by the continuity girl)'. The series' producer Peter Jones wrote to *The Sunday Telegraph* to convey the footage was entirely genuine. Wilson put his name to an apology conveying that he regretted misleading his readers.

- Three other major series were commissioned during the 1990s: *Life in the Freezer* (1993), a six-part series about Antarctic wildlife; *The Private Life of Plants* (1995) and *The Life of Birds* (1998).

- Critic A.N. Wilson, then of *The Independent*, wrote a column in 1993 to criticise the cruelty of the *Life in the Freezer* team. He thought a sequence of a leopard seal killing a baby Adélie penguin must have involved throwing baby penguins to the seal until they got the right shot. The series editor, Alastair Fothergill, threatened legal action. Wilson wrote a grovelling apology and *The Independent* offered a large sum in an out-of-court settlement, which was donated to the Falkland Island Conservation Society's penguin appeal.

- *The Life of Birds* (1998) took three years to make and involved travelling to 42 countries. David travelled 256,000 miles during its filming. Iconic moments included David being knocked over by a randy capercaillie and extraordinary footage of a lyrebird mimicking a camera shutter, chainsaw and car alarm. Tragically, David's wife Jane died during the filming, on the eve of their 47th wedding anniversary.

EMOTIONAL ROLLER COASTER

AFRICA EPISODE 2: 'SAVANNAH'

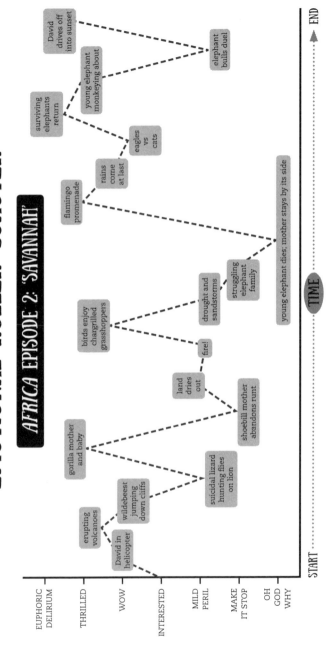

EUPHORIC
DELIRIUM

THRILLED

WOW

INTERESTED

MILD
PERIL

MAKE
IT STOP

OH
GOD
WHY

START

TIME

END

David in helicopter

erupting volcanoes

wildebeest jumping down cliffs

suicidal lizard hunting flies on lion

gorilla mother and baby

shoebill mother abandons runt

land dries out

fire!

birds enjoy chargrilled grasshoppers

drought and sandstorms

struggling elephant family

young elephant dies; mother stays by its side

flamingo promenade

rains come at last

eagles vs cats

surviving elephants return

young elephant monkeying about

David drives off into sunset

elephant bulls duel

FIND THE REAL SPECIES

Can you spot the real species lurking among this frankly ludicrous-sounding collection of animals?

1A Elf Shark
1B Goblin Shark
1C Orc Shark
1D Hobbit Shark

2A Giant Violinfish
2B Giant Violafish
2C Giant Guitarfish
2D Giant Cellofish

3A Paradoxical Frog
3B Contradictory Frog
3C Hyperbolic Frog
3D Antithetic Frog

4A Spotted Bathrobe Fish
4B Striped Negligee Fish
4C Spotted Bedclothes Fish
4D Striped Pyjama Fish

(Answers on page 190.)

GUESS THE ANIMALS

Can you guess the animals David's talking about?

1 *'According to folklore, it can eat more at one sitting than any other creature in the forest, hence its other name, the glutton.'*

A Three-toed Sloth
B Wolverine
C Grizzly Bear
D Javan Ferret-badger

2 *'At five miles down, this is the deepest living fish so far discovered. No one imagined that an animal as complex as a fish could exist in such extreme pressures.'*

A Frilled Shark
B Fangtooth Fish
C Six-gill Shark
D Ethereal Snailfish

3 *'So they observe strict rules in their fights which prohibit the use of their lethal bite. Slowed down, it's a performance full of grace as each contestant strives not to kill his opponent but simply to slam him to the ground.'*

A Mexican Beaded Lizard
B King Cobra
C Komodo Dragon
D Black Widow Spider

4 *'The vibrations in his body are so powerful they make the water dance along his back. Raising their backs slightly above the surface of the water is a significant move. It's a claim to dominance.'*

A American Alligator
B Common Hippopotamus
C Great White Shark
D California Sea Lion

5 *'This is the furthest these mighty giants now venture into Eastern Africa. They're marooned on their islands in the African sky.'*

A Tapanuli Orangutan
B Common Chimpanzee
C Bonobo
D Mountain Gorilla

6 *'They're tiny, each weighing the same as a couple of £1 coins, yet the journey to their breeding grounds in Europe is over 5,000 miles long.'*

A Barn Swallow
B Arctic Tern
C Bee Hummingbird
D Hummingbird Hawk Moth

7 *'In Egypt, the challenge is to get into the world of the most heat-tolerant desert animal. They're one of the fastest sprinters in the animal kingdom.'*

A Thorny Devil
B Deathstalker Scorpion
C Saharan Silver Ant
D Armadillo Girdled Lizard

8 *'They can raise their body temperature to 10 degrees above that of the surrounding sea. But doing so requires an enormous amount of high-grade fuel.'*

A Bottlenose Dolphin
B West Indian Manatee
C Basking Shark
D Great White Shark

(Answers on page 190.)

SPOT THE DIFFERENCE

Can you spot the seven differences
between this desert scene and the one opposite?

(Answers on
page 190.)

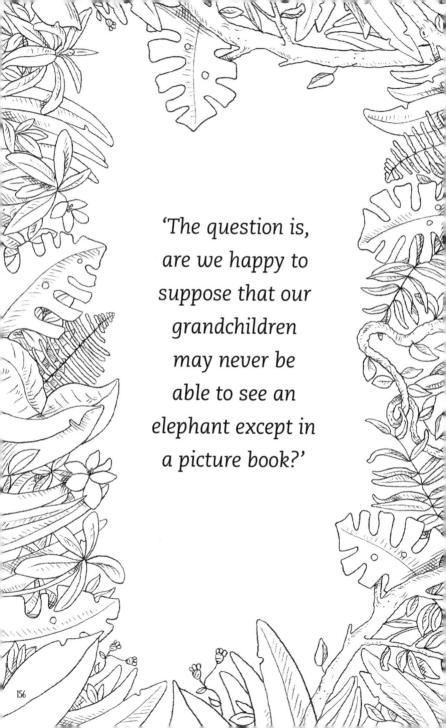

'The question is,
are we happy to
suppose that our
grandchildren
may never be
able to see an
elephant except in
a picture book?'

AFRICA
ENTIRE SERIES SCRIPT
WORD CLOUD

Africa
around animals
change away become chance
created creatures chick continent
desert earth eggs elephants
enough female fish food forest
going land life lions live male
miles million mother
mountain protect rain
reach really rhino
rivers sahara sand
sea seems sun
survive trees
turtles water
wild wildlife
world
years
young

COLOUR IN A HUMMINGBIRD!

OK, so full disclosure: I'm obsessed with hummingbirds. The fiery-throated hummingbird basically looks like it's been dipped into a rainbow. It has a red throat, which blends into orange and yellow on its chest. It has a green belly and a blue-green back that becomes indigo towards its rump. Its wings are violet. But you can colour it however you want!

ATTENBOROUGH FIELD NOTES
THE 2000s

- The 2000s saw David never far from our TV screens, with six major series appearing during this time: *The Blue Planet* (2001); *The Life of Mammals* (2002); *Life in the Undergrowth* (2005); *Planet Earth* (2006); *Life in Cold Blood* (2008); *Nature's Great Events* (2009) and *Life* (2009).

- *The Blue Planet* took nearly five years to produce and took the team to 200 shooting locations. More than 12 million people watched the eight-part series in the UK and it was sold to over 50 countries.

- *The Blue Planet* won two Emmy Awards and was nominated for a further three. It won two BAFTAs and was nominated for another four.

- Within a year of its release, *The Blue Planet* DVD had become the bestselling non-movie DVD of all time.

- *The Life of Mammals* involved several groundbreaking scenes including an adult blue whale surfacing next to David's boat. Technological advances meant that the team were able to use infrared cameras to film lions hunting zebras at night and watch as a leopard entered an Indian village searching for goats; in doing so it came very close to the hut David was observing from.

- The third episode of *The Life of Mammals* features David saying 'boo' to a sloth; the final episode includes footage of rescued orangutans that have learned to use tools including a hammer and a saw.

- *Planet Earth* took five years to make and was at the time the most expensive nature documentary ever produced by the BBC. It was the first to be filmed in high definition and was shown in over 130 countries.

- *Planet Earth* won multiple international awards including four Emmys and a Peabody Award. The first five episodes of the series attracted an average viewership of 11.4 million in the UK. It also performed well in the US, with the first three episodes drawing an average of 5.72 million.

- *Planet Earth* included the world's first video of snow leopards. Other iconic scenes included young polar bears emerging from their den and bottlenose dolphins inventing a 'hydroplaning' hunting technique in shallow waters. Infrared cameras were used to show a pride of lions hunting and killing an elephant.

CRITICALLY ENDANGERED AMPHIBIANS

There are 552 amphibians listed on the IUCN Red List of Threatened Species 2017 as 'Critically Endangered', including 373 frogs and 79 salamanders.

AMONG THE SALAMANDERS, THERE ARE:

8 members of the Ambystomatidae family (known as the mole salamanders) • **1** member of the Cryptobranchidae family (the Chinese Giant Salamander) • **5** members of the Hynobiidae family (known as the Asiatic salamanders) • **62** members of the Plethodontidae family (known as lungless salamanders) • **3** members of the Salamandridae family (the true salamanders and newts)

AMONG THE FROGS, THERE ARE:

13 members of the Telmatobidae family (water frogs) • **62** members of the Eleutherodactylidae family (robber or rain frogs) • **24** members of the Rhacophoridae family (shrub frogs) • **9** members of the Aromobatidae family (cryptic forest frogs) • **8** members of the Brevicipitidae family (rain frogs) • **100** members of the Bufonidae family (true toads) • **65** members of the Craugastoridae family (fleshbelly frogs) • **7** members of the Centrolenidae faily (glass frogs) • **6** members of the Megophryidae family (litter frogs) • **10** members of the Arthroleptidae family (sometimes known as screeching frogs) • **12** members of the Dendrobatidae family (poison dart frogs) • **13** members of the Mantellidae family (a group of diverse frogs from Madagascar and Mayotte) • **13** members of the Microhylidae family (narrow-mouthed frogs) • **11** members of the Ranidae family (true frogs) • **6** members of the Myobatrachidae family (Australian ground frogs) • **68** members of the Hylidae family (referred

to as tree frogs and allies) •
5 members of the Hyperoliidae
family (sometimes called African
reed frogs) • **4** members of
the Alsodidae family (small
family of frogs from South
America) • **1** member of the
Alytidae family (known as
painted frogs) • **1** member
of the Ceratobatrachidae family
(found in Malaysia, Thailand, Myanmar, Borneo,
Philippines, Palau, Fiji, New Guinea, Admiralty Islands,
Bismarck islands and Solomon Islands) • **1** member of
the Conrauidae family (sometimes called slippery frogs)
• **3** members of the Cycloramphidae family (only found
in southeastern Brazil) • **3** members of the Dicroglossidae
family (known as fork-tongued frogs) • **1** member of the
Heleophrynidae family (known as ghost frogs) • **3** members
of the Hemiphractidae family (found in South and Central
America) • **1** member of the Leiopelmatidae family (also
known as New Zealand primitive frogs) • **4** members of
the Leptodactylidae family (also called southern frogs)
• **1** member of the Limnodynastidae family (also called
Australian swamp frogs) • **1** member of the Micrixalidae
family (known as dancing frogs) • **1** member of the
Nyctibatrachidae family (known as night frogs) • **1** member
of the Odontophrynidae family (found in southern and
eastern South America) • **1** member of the Petropedetidae
family (sometimes called African torrent frogs) • **1** member
of the Phrynobatrachidae family (known as puddle frogs)
• **2** members of the Phyllomedusidae family (found in
Central and South America) • **2** members of the Pipidae
family (primitive tongueless frogs found in South America
and sub-Saharan Africa) • **4** members of the Pyxicephalidae
family (found in sub-Saharan Africa) • **2** members of the
Sooglossidae family (also called Seychelles frogs)

ATTENBOROUGH'S ARK

These are the ten species Sir David named to accompany him on his personal ark in 2012 for a BBC Two *Natural World* Special.

1 Black lion tamarin A small New World monkey named for the facial hair surrounding their faces.

2 Sumatran rhino The smallest of the five species of rhino.

3 Solenodon A burrowing mammal with a long flexible snout and venomous saliva.

4 Olm salamander A blind aquatic salamander that lives underground.

5 Marvellous spatuletail hummingbird White-, green- and bronze-coloured hummingbird with two long tail feathers that end with a racquet shape.

6 Darwin's frog Brown or green frog named after the man who discovered it during his voyage on HMS *Beagle* in the 1830s.

7 Sunda pangolin Endangered southeast Asian mammal with unique armoured scales.

8 Priam's birdwing butterfly Striking iridescent green and black butterfly.

9 Northern quoll Carnivorous marsupial native to Australia.

10 Venus's flower basket A type of deep-ocean sponge.

MATCH THE ANIMAL

MATCH THE FEMALE ANIMAL NAME TO THE ANIMAL

ANIMAL	FEMALE ANIMAL NAME
Armadillo	Duck
Cat	Mare
Elephant	Nanny
Fox	Molly
Goat	Vixen
Kangaroo	Cow
Leopard	Ewe
Mallard	Jenny
Mule	Queen
Parrot	Sow
Raccoon	Doe
Sheep	Pen
Squirrel	Hen
Swan	Jill
Wren	Female
Zebra	Leopardess

(Answers on page 190.)

MATCH THE ANIMAL

MATCH THE MALE ANIMAL NAME TO THE ANIMAL

ANIMAL	MALE ANIMAL NAME
Alligator	Ram
Badger	Hob
Bee	Cock
Chicken	Buck
Deer	Stallion
Duck	Jack
Falcon	Boar
Ferret	Reynard
Fox	Bull
Goose	Drone
Hare	Rooster
Horse	Gander
Hummingbird	Cob
Sheep	Drake
Swan	Stag
Wallaby	Tercel

(Answers on pages 190–191.)

WHERE'S DAVID?

Can you spot the world's most famous naturalist (in miniature) amid this urban scene?

ATTENBOROUGH FIELD NOTES
THE 2010s

- The last few years has witnessed some of the biggest BBC documentary series ever produced, including *Frozen Planet* (2011), *Africa* (2013), *Planet Earth II* (2016) and *Blue Planet II* (2017).

- *Frozen Planet* won three awards at the British Academy Television Craft Awards, for Sound, Photography and Editing.

- The second episode of *Frozen Planet* saw a UK viewership of 9.72 million, more than the most-watched episode of *Planet Earth*.

- *Frozen Planet*'s most memorable scenes included a criminal Adélie penguin stealing stones from his neighbour to build his own nest and young polar bears emerging from their burrow for the first time. There was also a particularly harrowing scene involving killer whales and a baby seal, but I'm not talking about that again.

- Alec Baldwin replaced David as the narrator for *Frozen Planet* in the US and Forest Whitaker filled David's shoes as the narrator for *Africa*.

- *Africa* brought viewers particularly heart-rending scenes, including a female elephant appearing to grieve over her dying calf and a mother shoebill leaving her weaker chick to die of starvation.

- *Planet Earth II* was the first television series that the BBC produced in 4K (ultra-high definition).

- *Planet Earth II*'s highest viewing figures were 13.14 million, eclipsing even *The Blue Planet*'s top figure of 12.01 million. It won the BAFTA's Huw Wheldon Award for Specialist Factual and the BAFTA's Must-See Moment Award for the famous snakes vs iguanas chase. It also took home the Emmy Awards for Outstanding Documentary or Nonfiction Series and for Cinematography.

- *Planet Earth II*'s iconic scenes included the spectacular snakes vs iguana chase; the back-scratching grizzly bear seemingly dancing to the song 'Jungle Boogie'; the bobcat face-planting in the snow; the amorous swimming sloth; the Mumbai leopards stalking the city by night; and the lion pride attempting to take down a giraffe.

- *Blue Planet II* was a sensation, reaching a record viewership of 14.01 million in the UK for episode one.

- *Blue Planet II*'s iconic scenes included a giant trevally fish jumping out of the water to catch a young Arctic tern, emperor penguins tiptoeing around sleeping elephant seals, and the horror movie-worthy Bobbit worm (named after the lady who severed a delicate part of her husband's anatomy) opening its terrifying jaws and dragging a fish into its burrow.

SPOT THE DIFFERENCE

Can you spot the seven differences between this urban scene and the one opposite?

(Answers on page 191.)

CRITICALLY ENDANGERED FISH

The 23 cartilaginous fish below feature on the IUCN Red List of Threatened Species 2017 as 'Critically Endangered'.

Angelshark • Brazilian Guitarfish • Caribbean Electric Ray • Common Skate • Daggernose Shark • Ganges Shark • Green Sawfish • Irrawaddy River Shark • Java Stingaree (species of stingray that is feared to be extinct but listed as critically endangered) • Largetooth Sawfish • Longnose Skate • Maltese Skate • Natal Shyshark • New Guinea River Shark • Ornate Sleeper Ray • Pakistan Whipray • Pondicherry Shark • Red Sea Torpedo (bottom-dwelling species of ray) • Sawback Angelshark • Smalltooth Sawfish • Smoothback Angelshark • Striped Smooth-hound (species of shark residing on the continental shelves off the coast of Brazil and Argentina) • Stripenose Guitarfish

There are a further **441** species of ray-finned fish (Actinopterygii) on the Critically Endangered List including the Beluga (European Sturgeon), Apache Trout, Valencia Toothcarp, Giant Salmon Carp, Andean Catfish, Mekong Giant Catfish, Chinese Bahaba, Giant Sea Bass, Southern Bluefin Tuna, European Eel and Chinese Puffer.

There are **2** members of the order *Petromyzontiformes* (a category of jawless fish comprising the lampreys) listed as Critically Endangered: the Greek Brook Lamprey and Mexican Lamprey.

There are **7** members of the *Cnidaria* phylum listed as Critically Endangered: Staghorn Coral, Elkhorn Coral, Floreana Coral, *Millepora boschmai* (a species of fire coral), *Porites pukoensis* (a species of stony coral), *Siderastrea glynni* (a species of reef-building stony coral) and Wellington's Solitary Coral.

There is **1** member of the Sarcopterygii (lobe-finned fish) class listed as Critically Endangered: the West Indian Ocean Coelacanth.

EMOTIONAL ROLLER COASTER

THE BLUE PLANET EPISODE 8: 'COASTS'

EUPHORIC DELIRIUM
THRILLED
WOW
INTERESTED
MILD PERIL
MAKE IT STOP
OH GOD WHY

START ...... TIME ...... END

diving marine iguanas
crashing waves
green turtles nesting
hawk vs iguana
Ridley's turtle hatchlings make it to the sea
baby turtle massacre
puffin city!
colossal seabird colony
mass fish suicide
sea eagle vs seagulls
surfing penguins
raven vs little auklets
sea lion torturing penguin
scavengers devour whale carcass
walruses lounging
sea lion family swimming lesson
elephant seals in bloody battle
killer whale attack
prolonged seal pup torture

173

WHERE'S DAVID?

Can you spot the world's most famous naturalist (in miniature) amid this mangrove landscape?

ATTENBOROUGH WORDSEARCH

ATTENBOROUGH'S ANIMALS

```
K A A F U C V M C O Z A T X N
Q V S L O T H K R A N G I Q A
J A I N L M D A U A U Z B Y C
C M I E J I N N U D J A B A J
P X W R C G R G O M X J O H H
X I V Q U H I O F L J O B C E
L A Z T G E I L G I B Z L Z B
K J A D N K W M W D J R A L L
F N U I S J U E P J J H P P U
J L R C A P E R C A I L L I E
F A B H X D L X E J N R V Q W
M J D R I B E R Y L U Z X J H
B K C Y F Q J H O M J C E N A
V X S L K S A L E S Y B S E L
F Z T K C P E L I V B Z S P E
```

BLUE WHALE   GORILLA

CHIMPANZEE   MARINE IGUANA

LYREBIRD   CAPERCAILLIE

SLOTH   LEMUR

BOBBIT   ORANGUTAN

(Answers on page 191.)

MERRY CHRISTMAS COLOURING-IN PAGE

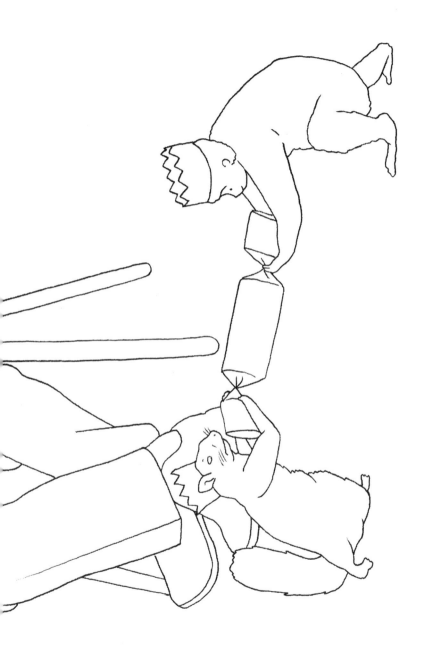

'Cherish the
natural world
because you're a
part of it and you
depend on it.'

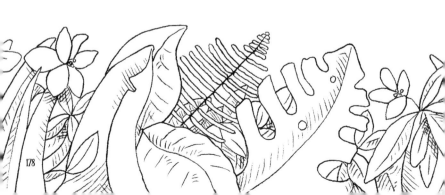

EMERGENCY APOLOGY NOTE

Please cut out in case of emergency and
immediately improve someone's day!

**I'm sorry I forgot your
birthday/graduation/wedding/
engagement party/moving-in party**

**Here's a picture of David Attenborough
to make you feel better**

THE ULTIMATE NATURE QUIZ!

1 Which animal's name means 'river horse' in Greek?

2 The northern cardinal is the state bird of seven US states. Can you name one of the states?

3 Hedwig, Harry Potter's owl, is which species of owl?

4 Lemurs can only be found on which island?

5 Charlie was the name of which creature that the *Zoo Quest* team brought back from Indonesia?

6 The giant panda is the logo for which environmental organisation?

7 The last male member of which species died in Kenya in 2011?

8 After the cheetah, what is the second-fastest cat?

9 A cross between a male tiger and a female lion is known as what?

10 The basilisk lizard is also known by which name for its ability to walk on water?

11 Black bears can run at speeds of up to (A) 25 mph, (B) 35 mph or (C) 45 mph?

12 The Latin name of which creature translates as 'tooth-walking sea horse'?

13 Megalodon is an extinct species of what?

14 A mudskipper can use its pectoral fins to do what unusual activity for a fish?

15 A parliament is the collective noun for which animal?

16 The four stages of a butterfly's life cycle are egg, larva, _____ and adult?

17 A squid has 8 arms but how many tentacles?

18 What is the name of a male bee?

19 What is the longest venomous snake? (A) reticulated python (B) king cobra (C) spitting cobra

20 Which flightless bird endemic to Mauritius became extinct approximately 300 years ago?

21 Which Central American country features an eagle and snake on its green, white and red flag?

22 Which Asian island nation's flag features a lion holding a blade?

23 Which African country's flag shows a grey crowned crane amid six horizontal bands of black, white and red?

24 The giant tortoise is endemic to which island archipelago?

25 The only wild monkey population in Europe exists in which British Overseas Territory?

26 Which marine creature has the heaviest brain, at 8kg? **(A)** killer whale **(B)** whale shark **(C)** sperm whale

27 Which is the largest species of penguin? **(A)** king penguin **(B)** gentoo penguin **(C)** emperor penguin

28 An insect body comprises the head, abdomen and which part?

29 Are there more species of birds or ants?

30 What colour is the blood of a spider?

31 Ophidiophobia is the fear of which cold-blooded creature?

32 Which is the only family of birds that can fly backwards?

33 In *Planet Earth II*, which species of big cat was filmed stalking the city of Mumbai by night?

34 Sidewinding is a form of locomotion unique to which animals?

35 The first episode of *Planet Earth II* included a spectacular scene of racer snakes pursuing which species of lizard?

36 Theresa May presented the leader of China, Xi Jinping, with a box set of which David Attenborough series in February 2018?

37 Which was the world's first national park?

38 Which famous sandstone rock formation is also known as Uluru?

39 Which mountain is also known as Mount Godwin-Austen?

40 Mount St Helens is located in which northwestern US state?

41 Eyjafjallajökull is a volcano located in which country?

42 Which geologic period followed the Jurassic?

43 Dippy the Diplodocus was an iconic feature of which famous building?

44 Which bird of prey species was successfully reintroduced in England between 1989 and 1994?

45 Dzanga Bai is a huge clearing in central Africa associated with which animal?

46 Only male mosquitoes bite – true or false?

47 Lord Byron famously kept an unusual pet while studying at Cambridge University. What was it? **(A)** a raccoon **(B)** a bear **(C)** a parrot

48 Which nautical-sounding Madagascan animal is the only primate that uses echolocation to find food?

49 A giraffe's neck weighs approximately how many kilograms? **(A)** 70 **(B)** 170 **(C)** 270

50 Charles Darwin commenced a five-year voyage on which ship in 1831?

51 What colour is a polar bear's skin? **(A)** brown **(B)** white **(C)** black

52 The last known Pinta Island tortoise died in 2012. What name was he known by?

53 What lives in compact colonies of many identical individual polyps?

54 The largest bird's egg weighed 2.589kg, but which bird species laid it?

55 The oldest continuously operating zoo in the world opened in which city in 1752?

56 All scorpions have a venomous sting – true or false?

57 David famously witnessed the migration of millions of crabs in *Trials of Life*, but which island do they hail from?

58 What is the only mammal capable of sustained flight?

59 What is the name of a young swan?

60 A firefly is a species of which creature?

61 Glow-worms and fireflies are capable of producing light, but what is the scientific term for this phenomenon?

62 The secretary bird is famously capable of hunting what type of creature?

63 Which bird possesses the longest wingspan?

64 Jane Goodall is associated with the study of which species of primate?

65 What is the two-word scientific term for the Northern Lights?

66 Which bird of prey is the national animal of several South American nations?

67 What is the largest living reptile? **(A)** saltwater crocodile **(B)** Komodo dragon **(C)** leatherback sea turtle

68 An owl can move its head up to how many degrees in either direction? **(A)** 230 **(B)** 250 **(C)** 270

69 What is the largest native mammal in the UK?

70 The Shakespeare play *The Winter's Tale* includes the famous stage direction, 'Exit pursued by a _____'?

71 The kakapo is a species of which bird family?

72 How many hearts does an octopus have? **(A)** 3 **(B)** 4 **(C)** 5

73 The peregrine falcon is recorded as the fastest bird in the world, but which bird is the second fastest?

74 Edgar Allan Poe wrote the famous poem 'The Raven', but which writer's pet bird was the poem inspired by?

75 An electric eel can deliver a shock of up to how many volts? **(A)** 240 **(B)** 480 **(C)** 600

76 Which mammal has the longest gestation period?

77 The male of this Australian animal is called a boomer and the female a flyer. Name that species!

78 A duck-billed platypus is capable of producing venom – true or false?

79 Australia has 21 of the world's 25 most venomous species of what?

80 Which ocean-dwelling creature was confirmed to have hunted and killed great white sharks off the coast of South Africa in 2017?

81 Which is the second largest shark, after the whale shark?

82 The venus flytrap is a carnivorous plant endemic to which continent?

83 What is the largest reptile species in Africa?

84 What is the name of the wild horses of the American west?

85 Hyperion is the name of the tallest living tree, measuring 380 feet, but is it a giant sequoia or a coast redwood?

86 Some species of hummingbird can beat their wings approximately how many times per second? **(A)** 60 **(B)** 80 **(C)** 100

87 Adult monarch butterflies only feed on what food source?

88 Which common gamebird was naturalised in Great Britain around AD1059?

89 Which family of lizards are known for their abilty to move each eye independently?

90 What is the name of the nest a squirrel builds?

91 A vespiary is the name of the nest of which creature?

92 Which bird is known for its ability to hunt cooperatively in packs?

93 A starfish possesses a remarkable ability to do what with its stomach?

94 How many different waterfalls comprise Niagara Falls? **(A)** 3 **(B)** 10 **(C)** 30

95 What is the common name for a tornado over water?

96 A rhumba is the collective noun for which species of snake?

97 What is the widest river in the world?

98 Melittology is the study of which animal?

99 Which migratory bird is also known as the sea swallow?

100 A human has seven vertebrae – how many does a giraffe have?

(Answers on page 191.)

THANK YOU, DAVID

David writes back to viewer's letters, so why not compose
a letter to him on this page? We've left the reverse blank so
you can cut the page out and send it off to him, c/o the BBC!

ANSWER PAGES

PAGES 10–11 GUESS THE ANIMALS

1B Komodo Dragon
2A Giant Cuttlefish
3B Andean Flamingo
4A Draco (Flying) Lizard
5D Golden Mole
6D Three-toed Sloth
7A Sperm Whale
8A Giraffe

PAGE 15 PUZZLES

1. 6 letters: J, P, Q, W, X, Y
2. The calls of a superb lyrebird from *Life of Birds*

PAGE 26 ATTENBOGGLE

There are 94 words of four or more letters on this board. However, I'm only going to accept the 42 of them shown below because the others are the sort of words that families argue over, then someone gets a dictionary out and it gets ugly. Five bonus points for getting otter.

abort	ever	ogre	tough
avert	goer	onto	tree
batter	gore	**otter**	trot
bon	gotta	rota	trough
bore	gree	rotate	unto
bough	greet	rote	veer
bunt	grot	rough	vert
data	hobo	tore	veto
date	hotter	tort	vetoer
dater	natter	torte	
ergo	oboe	tote	

PAGE 32 FIND THE REAL SPECIES?

1C White-bellied Go-away Bird
2A Dik-dik (a species of small antelope that lives in the bushlands of southern and Eastern Africa)
3A Agra Cadabra (a species of Amazonian beetle)
4B Satanic Leaf–tailed Gecko

PAGES 52–53 GUESS THE ANIMALS

1B Butcherbird
2D Sunfish
3C Bobbit
4C Marine Iguana
5B Portuguese Man o' War
6A Great Bowerbird
7A African Elephant
8D Naked Mole Rat

PAGE 64 DAVID NEVER UTTERS A CROSS WORD

Across	Down
2. King Cobra	**1.** Indian
5. Ostrich	**3.** Chimpanzee
6. Mariana	**4.** Ammonite
8. Jaguar	**7.** Jackal
11. Orca	**9.** Emperor
12. Red Admiral	**10.** Manatee
14. Drone	**13.** Krill

PAGE 75 MATCH THE ANIMAL

Animal	Nest Name
Seal	Rookery
Ant	Formicary
Rabbit	Warren
Squirrel	Drey
Otter	Holt
Beaver	Lodge
Eagle	Eyrie
Badger	Sett
Hare	Form
Pheasant	Nide

Animal	Adjective
Otter	Lutrine
Snake	Serpentine
Crow	Corvine
Moth	Lepidopterous
Turtle	Chelonian
Bear	Ursine
Fox	Vulpine
Horse	Equine
Eagle	Aquiline
Bee	Apian

PAGE 78 PUZZLES

No extra points for sequels/prequels/remakes. I'm not accepting *Antz* because the 'z' is frankly unacceptable. If you name a film that isn't in the list below, then well done. Give yourself a point and enjoy the feeling of being even more of a nerd than me.

12 Monkeys; 101 Dalmatians; The African Lion; Alligator; Alvin and the Chipmunks; Anaconda; Ant-Man; Babe: Pig in the City; Batman; Big Fish; The Birds; Black Hawk Down; Black Swan; Brother Bear; The Butterfly Effect; The Cat in the Hat; Cat on a Hot Tin Roof; Cats & Dogs; The Chronicles of Narnia: The Lion, The Witch and the Wardrobe; Coyote Ugly; Crocodile Dundee; Crouching Tiger, Hidden Dragon; The Crow; Dances with Wolves; The Day of the Jackal; The Deer Hunter; The Diving Bell and the Butterfly; Dog Day Afternoon; Dog Soldiers; Duck Soup; The Elephant Man; Fantastic Mr Fox; A Fish Called Wanda; Fish Tank; The Fly; Four Lions; The Fox and the Hound; Gorillas in the Mist; The Great Mouse Detective; Hatchi: A Dog's Tale; G.I. Joe: The Rise of Cobra; Groundhog Day; Howard the Dog; Ice Station Zebra; Kangaroo Jack; Kiss of the Spider Woman; Kung Fu Panda; The Lion King; The Maltese Falcon; March of the Penguins; Mighty Ducks; The Mouse that Roared; Must Love Dogs; Night of the Iguana; Of Mice and Men; One Flew Over the Cuckoo's Nest; Orca: The Killer Whale; The Pelican Brief; The Pink Panther; Piranha; Planet of the Apes; Rabbit-proof Fence; Raging Bull; Rat Race; Reservoir Dogs; Save the Tiger; Scorpion King; Shark Tale; Shooting Fish; The Silence of the Lambs; Snake Eyes; Snakes on a Plane; Spider Man; Straw Dogs; Tarantula; Teen Wolf; To Kill a Mockingbird; The Truth About Cats and Dogs; Wag the Dog; The Water Horse; Where Eagles Dare; The Wings of the Dove; Whale Rider; Who Framed Roger Rabbit?; Wolf; Wolf Creek; X-Men Origins: Wolverine

PAGES 86 MATCH THE ANIMAL

Animal	Collective Noun
Apes	Shrewdness
Bats	Colony
Butterflies	Kaleidoscope
Cockroaches	Intrusion
Crocodiles	Bask
Crows	Murder
Eagles	Convocation
Ferrets	Business
Finches	Charm
Flamingoes	Flamboyance
Foxes	Skulk
Grasshoppers	Cloud
Hyenas	Cackle
Larks	Exaltation
Locusts	Plague
Moles	Labour
Owls	Parliament
Parrots	Pandemonium
Peacocks	Ostentation
Pheasants	Bouquets
Porcupines	Prickle
Ravens	Unkindness
Rhinos	Crash
Salamanders	Maelstrom
Seagulls	Quabble
Sharks	Shiver
Starlings	Murmuration
Swifts	Cream
Vultures	Wake
Woodpeckers	Descent

PAGES 88–89 SPOT THE DIFFERENCE

Tree snake coil, fern leaf (upper right-hand side), monkey nostril, flower pistil, frog toe, leopard spot, markings on toucan bill.

PAGE 91 FIND THE REAL SPECIES

1A Sarcastic Fringehead (small aggressive fish with a very large mouth)
2B Sparklemuffin (a member of the Australian jumping spider family)
3C Raspberry Crazy Ant
4A Pink Fairy Armadillo

PAGE 100 MATCH THE ANIMAL

Animal	Baby Animal Name
Alligator	Hatchling
Antelope	Calf
Bat	Pup
Cicada	Nymph
Deer	Fawn
Dove	Squab
Ferret	Kit
Goat	Kid
Goose	Gosling
Gorilla	Infant
Hare	Leveret
Horse	Foal
Kangaroo	Joey
Lemur	Baby

Oyster......... Spat
Partridge......... Cheeper
Platypus......... Puggle
Rabbit......... Kitten
Swan......... Cygnet
Turkey......... Poult

PAGES 102-103 GUESS THE ANIMALS

1B Black Rhinoceros
2C African Rock Python
3A Galapagos Tortoise
4D Panamanian Golden Frog
5B Sifaka
6A Barn Owl
7D Atlas Beetle
8C Sword-billed Hummingbird

PAGES 104-105 SPOT THE DIFFERENCE

Zebra stripe, bird in the distance (above mountain), giraffe marking (on neck), tree branch (upper right-hand side), hyena marking, long grass stem (between hyena and wildebeest), lion tail.

PAGE 113 MATCH THE ANIMAL

Animal........Baby Animal Name
Butterfly........Caterpillar
Camel........Calf
Cat........Kitten
Cheetah........Cub
Donkey........Foal
Fly........Maggot
Goat........Kid
Grasshopper........Nymph
Hawk........Eyas
Hedgehog........Piglet
Heron........Chick
Llama........Cria
Mole ....Pup
Monkey........Infant
Peafowl........Peachick
Skunk........Kit
Spider........Spiderling
Toad........Tadpole
Trout........Fingerling
Wallaby........Joey

PAGE 116 FIND THE REAL SPECIES

1B Ice Cream Cone Worms
2B Strange-tailed Tyrant
3A Fried Egg Jellyfish
4C Pacific Spiny Lumpsucker

PAGE 122 ATTENBOROUGH WORDSEARCH

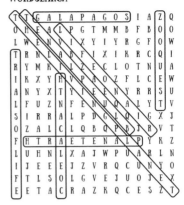

PAGE 127 DAVID NEVER UTTERS A CROSS WORD

Across
2. Kiwi
4. Groundhog
8. Vulnerable
9. Papua New Guinea
12. Richmond
13. Bald Eagle
14. Frederick

Down
1. Rwanda
3. Roadrunner
5. Galapagos
6. Greenpeace
7. Madagascar
10. Adder
11. Beagle

PAGES 132-133 ANIMAL ANAGRAMS

Toast (stoat)
Soot cup (octopus)
Torte (otter)
Paroled (leopard)
Tutor (trout)
Balancer (barnacle)
Greet (egret)
Unfolder (flounder)
Maniac (caiman)
Girls tan (starling)
Loo etc (ocelot)
Straying (stingray)
Storey (oyster)
Quits moo (mosquito)
Skelter (kestrel)
Neat tear (anteater)
Seal we (weasel)
Heats pan (pheasant)
Raptor (parrot)
Brisk pong (springbok)
Teach he (cheetah)

Plane toe (antelope)
Throne (hornet)
Long pain (pangolin)
Orca con (raccoon
Tailor lag (alligator)
Emanate (manatee)
Radio mall (armadillo)
Sandier (sardine)
Olive wren (wolverine)
Emitter (termite)
Oscar ways (cassowary)
Chained (echidna
Carrot nom (cormorant)
Leg laze (gazelle)
Upper coin (porcupine)
Trash me (hamster)
Dreams alan (salamander)
Fear fig (giraffe)
Impeach zen (chimpanzee)

PAGE 135 ATTENBOGGLE

There are 268 words of four or more letters on this board. However, I'm only going to accept the 123 of them shown below because the others are the sort of words that families argue over, then someone gets a dictionary out and it gets ugly. Five bonus points for getting each of the animals: **ants**, **stoat** and **rail**.

aero	errata	neutron	rots
aileron	lane	nona	ruer
alert	lean	none	ruers
alerts	leant	nonrural	rural
altar	learn	oral	rust
altars	learnt	**rail**	ruts
anal	lear	railer	**stoat**
annal	lears	raita	stone
anno	leer	rant	stoner
anon	lent	rants	store
anti	lentil	rattan	storer
antler	liar	real	strait
antlers	liars	rear	strats
ants	naan	rears	suer
area	nail	reearn	sure
arear	nailer	reel	surreal
arena	nailers	reliant	tail
arts	nana	relit	tailer
earn	natal	renal	tailers
ears	near	renail	tale
errant	nears	rent	talent
elan	neat	rental	talents
entail	neural	rents	tanner
entrail	neuron	rerail	tanners
errant	neutral	reran	tarot

tarots	tillers	torn	tree
tars	tone	torrent	truer
tart	toner	torrential	turner
tarts	toners	trail	urnal
tile	tonne	trait	urnal
tiler	tore	treat	

PAGE 151 FIND THE REAL SPECIES

1B Goblin Shark
2C Giant Guitarfish
3A Paradoxical Frog
4D Striped Pyjama Fish

PAGES 152-153 GUESS THE ANIMALS

1B Wolverine
2D Ethereal Snailfish
3B King Cobra
4A American Alligator
5D Mountain Gorilla
6A Barn Swallow
7C Saharan Silver Ant
8D Great White Shark

PAGES 154-155 SPOT THE DIFFERENCE

Meerkat paw, cactus stem (on horizon), llama leg, snake marking, lizard tail, camel knee, grass stem (front left-hand side).

PAGE 165 MATCH THE ANIMAL

Animal........Female Animal Name
Armadillo........Doe
Cat........Queen
Elephant........Cow
Fox........Vixen
Goat........Nanny
Kangaroo........Jill
Leopard........Leopardess
Mallard........Duck
Mule........Molly
Parrot........Hen
Raccoon........Sow
Sheep........Ewe
Squirrel........Doe
Swan........Pen
Wren........Jenny
Zebra........Mare

PAGE 166 MATCH THE ANIMAL

Animal........Male Animal Name
Alligator........Bull
Badger........Boar
Bee........Drone
Chicken........Rooster

Deer........Stag
Duck........Drake
Falcon........Tercel
Ferret........Hob
Fox........Reynard
Goose........Gander
Hare........Buck
Horse........Stallion
Hummingbird........Cock
Sheep........Ram
Swan........Cob
Wallaby........Jack

PAGES 170-171 SPOT THE DIFFERENCE

High-rise window, pigeon (middle left-hand side), crow leg, street lamp bulb, rat tail, hedgehog ear, starling tail.

PAGE 175 ATTENBOROUGH WORDSEARCH

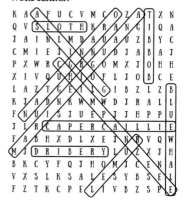

PAGES 180-184 THE ULTIMATE NATURE QUIZ

1. Hippopotamus
2. Illinois, Indiana, Kentucky, North Carolina, Ohio, Virginia and West Virginia
3. Snowy Owl
4. Madagascar
5. Orangutan
6. WWF (World Wide Fund for Nature)
7. Western Black Rhino
8. Lion
9. Tigon
10. Jesus Christ Lizard
11. (B) 35mph
12. Walrus
13. Shark
14. Walk on land
15. Owl
16. Pupa
17. 2
18. Drone
19. (B) King Cobra
20. Dodo
21. Mexico
22. Sri Lanka
23. Uganda
24. The Galapagos Islands
25. Gibraltar
26. (C) Sperm Whale
27. (C) Emperor Penguin
28. Thorax
29. Birds (approx. 9,000 species compared with 8,800 species of ant)
30. Blue
31. Snakes
32. Hummingbirds
33. Leopard
34. Snakes
35. Marine Iguana
36. Blue Planet II
37. Yellowstone, USA
38. Ayers Rock
39. K2
40. Washington
41. Iceland
42. Cretaceous
43. The Natural History Museum
44. Red Kite
45. Forest Elephants
46. False, it's just the females!
47. (B) a bear
48. Aye-Aye
49. (C) 270
50. HMS Beagle
51. (C) black
52. Lonesome George
53. Coral
54. Ostrich
55. Vienna
56. True
57. Christmas Island
58. Bat
59. Cygnet
60. Beetle
61. Bioluminescence
62. Snakes
63. Wandering Albatross
64. Chimpanzees
65. Aurora Borealis
66. Andean Condor
67. (A) Saltwater Crocodile
68. (C) 270
69. Red Deer
70. Bear
71. Parrot
72. (A) 3
73. Golden Eagle
74. Charles Dickens
75. (C) 600
76. Elephant
77. Kangaroo
78. True
79. Snake
80. Killer Whale (Orca)
81. Basking Shark
82. North America
83. Nile Crocodile
84. Mustangs
85. Coast Redwood
86. (B) 80
87. Nectar
88. Pheasant
89. Chameleons
90. Drey
91. Wasp
92. Harris Hawks
93. Ejecting its stomach from its body in order to feed
94. (A) 3
95. Waterspout
96. Rattlesnake
97. Amazon
98. Bees
99. Arctic Tern
100. Also 7!

ACKNOWLEDGEMENTS

First and foremost, to the great man himself, Sir David Attenborough. The world is an infinitely better place for your wisdom, passion, courage, humour and kindness.

To my wife Tarah, for believing that I can do anything I put my mind to. I'd be an absolute shambles without you!
To Deborah Burgess, music consultant, sounding board and knower of lingo.
To Steph Milner for believing that this ludicrous idea might be quite funny.

A big thank you to the delightful folk at Pavilion for your enthusiasm.
Nicola – you've been a star, and this has been a wonderful adventure.
Gemma and Sally – thank you for your tireless, terrific work.
And many thanks to Tina and David for your support and passion for the project.

Finally to Peter James Field for bringing the book to life in stunning fashion.